D. Eric Maikranz

Times Editions
Marshall Cavendish

In the same series:
Frankfurt
Kuala Lumpur
Rome
Singapore
Tokyo

© 2005 Marshall Cavendish International (Asia) Private Limited

Editor: Katharine Brown-Carpenter
Designer: Benson Tan
Map Illustrator: Ang Lee Pheng

Published by Times Editions—Marshall Cavendish
An imprint of Marshall Cavendish International (Asia) Private Limited
A member of Times Publishing Limited
Times Centre, 1 New Industrial Road, Singapore 536196
Tel: (65) 6213 9300   Fax: (65) 6285 4871
E-mail: te@sg.marshallcavendish.com
Online Bookstore: http://www.marshallcavendish.com/genref

National Library Board Singapore Cataloguing in Publication Data
Maikranz, D. Eric (David Eric), 1967–.
Insider's Venice / D. Eric Maikranz. — Singapore : Times Editions-Marshall Cavendish, c2005.
p. cm.
Includes bibliographical references and index.
ISBN : 981-232-945-5
1. Venice (Italy)— History. 2. Venice (Italy)—Description and travel.
3. Venice (Italy)—Guidebooks. I. Title.
DG672.2
945.31—dc21   SLS2005025387

Printed and bound in Singapore

PHOTO CREDITS
All photographs by D. Eric Maikranz with the exception of the following: Corel: 14

Dedication

For Desiree, my wife, my partner and my friend

Contents

Foreword

Thank you for picking up this book, I promise you won't be disappointed. As you consider a guidebook to Venice, I urge you to continue reading this brief introduction to see if *Insider's Venice* meets your needs.

Insider's Venice is a unique effort when it comes to guidebooks to the city the locals call *la serenissima*, or 'the most serene'. There are many guidebooks available that offer hotel and restaurant listings as well as brief insight into the historical sites you will see in Venice. Likewise there are many good books describing the history and intrigues of Venice that fully engage you to the places you visit (remember that you visit Venice for the history and the architecture, not for the beach). *Insider's Venice* delivers both the historical background you need to make a visit meaningful and memorable as well as provides comprehensive listings for quaint hotels, local restaurants, out-of-the-way museums and churches and transportation facts to get you around quickly. The *Insider's* guidebooks are written by travellers for travellers who want more than what standard guides offer.

I wrote this book for two audiences. The first consists of travellers who thrive on the history and intrigue of the place they visit. These are the type of people who want to know the history of Casanova and his trial before the Inquisition before they visit the cell in which he was held. These travellers yearn to learn about Lord Byron's adventures in Venice rather than simply hear that he lived in a particular palazzo. They want to have the advantage of understanding why Veronese was arrested for producing an artwork instead of simply admiring it. For these travellers, merely following the tourist trail, taking some keepsake photographs and running off to see the next thing is not enough. They wish to bond with the city, to experience it on a deeper level. They want more than the standard guide provides and this book will deliver Venice over fully to them.

The second audience is made up of travellers who, unfortunately, will have only enough time in the city to take in the must-see sights and often journey throughout Italy or even all of Europe with a single large guidebook. While these ambitious travellers should be applauded for their energy and zeal, I would encourage them to take this book along as well in order to maximise their limited time in Venice. Passing through St. Mark's Basilica and admiring the mosaics and the tomb of St. Mark, the reader of this book will know that the church might have just as easily been called St. Theodore's and that the body of St. Mark is actually a stolen good. Standing in awe of Tintoretto's talent inside the Scuola Grande di San Rocco, readers of this book can chuckle at the deft trick the artist played on his rivals in order to gain the initial commission. A deeper appreciation of Venice's colourful history can only enrich their time in the city and, regardless of scheduling constraints, *Insider's Venice* will take them there.

But travellers cannot live on sights and history alone; therefore, we have included listings for quaint hotels, local restaurants, hip bars and local (affordable) shops. Each section, or neighbourhood, in the book has an author's list of recommendations that features the best Venice has to offer. The recommendations in this book are truly lists of my favourites in Venice. I hope you will enjoy them as much as I do.

Enjoy Venice!

D. Eric Maikranz

Introduction to the City

Venice—with its canals, gondolas, picturesque palazzos and magnificent St. Mark's Square—is one of the most popular tourist destinations in the world. The Jewel of the Adriatic for nearly fifteen centuries, waterborne Venice wows you every time. More than any other place in the world, Venice is truly a museum city where every building is a masterpiece, worthy of admiration.

The entire Venetian lagoon is listed as a World Heritage Site and it is easy to see why when walking around the city or taking an aquatic form of transportation. Venice is a great city to explore on foot. With no automobile traffic to speak of, the only obstacles for pedestrians are other walkers and the ubiquitous dog droppings. One of the best ways to spend a day in Venice is to walk around trying to get lost (don't worry it won't take long) and discover something new off the beaten track.

One of the biggest complaints people have upon visiting Venice is that it is too touristy, meaning that the city has capitalised on its importance as a tourist city in recent years and that this change is somehow distasteful. Well, I hate to let you down but Venice has been regarded as a city for tourists since the early 1700s. The truth of the matter is that Venice is good at whatever it decides to do. When it wanted to be a trading giant, it was the commercial centre of the Mediterranean. When it wanted to be a maritime power, it ruled the waves. Now it is simply selling the most valuable commodity it has, namely itself. And with typical Venetian style, it is doing it well. Don't worry, with this book to guide you, there is still plenty of native Venice left to explore away from the crowds.

Which brings me to my next point—crowds. Venice can be a very crowded place, especially in peak season (Carnival and September to October). Although the population of Venice is roughly 65,000, it is not unusual to have twice that number of tourists in the city. As a result, the pedestrian streets of Venice, especially the area around San Marco, can become choked with foot traffic and the *Vaporetti* (the ferry boat transportation system) are often standing room only. Your fellow travellers won't mind so much, but the outnumbered locals might let you hear about it if you insist on transporting luggage or slinging large backpacks around during peak travel times. Be considerate and tread lightly.

Modern Venetians speak Italian but it was not always the case. Venice, like most cities in Italy, used to have its own dialect. This dialect was unique in that it contracted many words and often dropped vowel endings. Only elderly Venetians speak this dialect today but its contractions and clipped words are carried over to street names, which might seem quite odd to Italian speakers. Most Venetians speak some English (and often other languages as well) as the city's stock and trade is accommodating outsiders.

Venice is notorious for its restaurants and many people complain that it is difficult to get a decent meal in the city. Well, these people never frequented the places in this book. Venice, with proper guidance, is a fine city for restaurants, especially if you like seafood. Try some distinctly Venetian dishes like spaghetti in squid ink (sublime) and freshly prepared *conche* (mantis prawns). One trip to the morning fish market at the Pescheria will let you know that everything served at better restaurants is that morning's catch.

Venice is a shopper's paradise and to many rivals the city's more traditional sights as the main draw. Gucci, Bruno Magli, Fendi, Armani, Bvlgari…the list goes on. Basically, if you want it, you can get it in Venice. The areas around San Marco are the most chic and the most expensive. Things become much more reasonable the further out you go. See the Insider's Tips section at the end of each chapter for further shopping details.

When it comes to the sights of Venice, most people take in St. Mark's Basilica, St. Mark's Square, the Doge's Palace and the Gallerie dell'Accademia. While these are certainly on the must-see list, the many churches of Venice are the true art museums as they house many works by such greats as Titian, Tintoretto, Veronese, Palma and Carpaccio. As a rule of thumb, I recommend to all visitors to enter any church they see open because it will contain something worth seeing. But the can't-miss churches are San Sebastiano, San Rocco, Santa Maria Gloriosa dei Frari (the Frari) and Santi Giovanni e Paolo (San Zanipolo).

Travel Facts

Climate

There are good times to visit Venice and not so good times. People often visualise Italy as a sunny paradise all year round. The truth is, on average, Venice gets 25.4–30.5 centimetres (10–12 inches) more rain per year than London. The trick is to know when to go. Venice is beautiful from April to June and from September to October. The rain begins in earnest at the end of October and continues until March. It snows about once every other year. August is prohibitively hot, with most Venetians abandoning the city for beach resorts. As a result, it is often difficult to locate open shops, hotels and restaurants in the city during the month of August. The stagnant canals are at their most ripe during August, too.

Flooding

Venice floods regularly but the locals take it in their stride and you should do the same. There are elevated walkways in the lowest areas of the city where flooding is worst (and occurs first). These walkways allow access to most areas and almost all the sights around San Marco. If a high flood is expected, i.e., over 1 metre (3.28 feet), an alarm siren sounds in St. Mark's Square several hours before the event. If the waters rise above 120 centimetres (47 inches), local police remove sections of the elevated walkway for safety reasons, namely the wooden planks of the walkway can float away. Many shops around San Marco carry a large supply of wellington boots or plastic overshoes that can do at a pinch. Flooding in Venice can happen anytime during the year but is most common and most pronounced in November and December.

Currency

Italy converted to the euro with eleven other European countries in 2002. Currency exchange offices and kiosks are conveniently located throughout the city. They are quite reputable and offer rates as good as or better than most banks. They definitely offer better hours and service as most Italian banks are open from 9am–1pm and 3pm–4.30pm and you will most likely stand in a queue for an hour at least. Using ATMs in Italy to access accounts in your home country also works well. Simply find a Cirrus or Plus network ATM, enter your card and pin and your currency will be dispensed in local euros. The conversion rates are good and almost all ATMs have an English-language option. Your bank may charge you for every international transaction that you make. Brand-name traveller's cheques (American Express, Thomas Cook, etc.) are still accepted at larger restaurants and hotels but expect to pay a service fee for cashing them.

Transportation

There are four ways to arrive in Venice: via the airport, train, motor vehicle and by sea. Marco Polo International Airport is located on the mainland just 13 kilometres (8 miles) from Venice. There is a free shuttle bus (Shuttle Darsena-Aerostazione) that stops in front of the airport and goes to the boat launch for water taxis (expensive) and the Alilaguna ferry to Venice (San Marco). Alilaguna has two lines (red and blue) that provide daily services to and from the airport and the city. The red line connects the airport to Murano Museo, Lido, Arsenale, San Marco and Zattere. The blue line connects the airport to Murano Colonna, Fondamenta Nuove, Lido, San Zaccaria, San Marco and Stazione Marittima (Maritime Station). The ferry costs Euro 5–13 depending on where you get off (Euro 10 to San Marco). Purchasers of the VENICECard (*see* Discount Opportunities below) can add a round trip from the airport to Venice for a small fee. Alternatively, two bus services link the airport with Venice (Piazzale Roma). The blue ATVO bus costs Euro 3 for a single journey and takes 20 minutes. It has luggage compartments where you can stow your bags. The No. 5 orange Actv bus takes a little longer as it picks up and drops off passengers between the airport and Piazzale Roma. It costs Euro 1 but there is an additional charge for large pieces of luggage. There are also no luggage racks on the bus.

Those travelling by train arrive at Stazione Santa Lucia on the western side of Venice. The station is just a few metres from the Grand Canal. Vaporetto stops (*see* Getting Around) are right out front. Travellers coming by car or bus arrive at the Piazzale Roma Car Park and Bus Station, which is on the western part of the island next to the train station. Seafarers arrive at Stazione Marittima next to both the Piazzale Roma Car Park and the train station.

Getting Around

There are two ways to get around in Venice—on foot and on the water. Walking is the best way to get around. The city itself is not really that big. Walking across the island from the train station to the edges of Castello will take about 90 minutes. Walking also accentuates the sereneness of Venice and makes you feel like you are really experiencing a unique place in the world.

The second way to get around is on the water, and here you have a couple of options. The first option is the Vaporetti, Venice's answer to public buses. Vaporetti, named after the vapour they emitted back in the days when they were steam-powered, service the main thoroughfares of the city: the Grand Canal, circumferential routes and routes to the outlying islands of the Lido, Murano, Burano, etc. Vaporetti are efficient ways to cover long distances but they can be expensive as a single use ticket will set you back Euro 3.50. A one-day return ticket costs Euro 6 and is valid until midnight on the day it is stamped. The fare for a shuttle journey from one stop to the next across the Grand Canal is Euro 1.80. Tickets to the outlying islands cost Euro 8.50. These tickets can be purchased at the booths near the stops and at local tobacco stores or newsstands. These costs can be mitigated with the purchase of a VENICECard or a transport pass (*see* Discount Opportunities below).

The next option is the water taxi. These lovely boats, 1950s vintage and Cris-Craft style, don't come cheap. The drop is Euro 9 and it increments at Euro 1.50 per minute. (It adds up very quickly, bearing in mind that Venice has tightly regulated speed limits that fall within single digits.)

Then there is the gondola, that most distinctive of Venetian vessels. Gondolas used to be the common form of transportation in the city, then they became the vessels of the rich. Today, they are the vessel of the tourist. Still, no trip to Venice is complete without having travelled

A solitary gondola makes its way along a quiet back canal, away from the hustle of the Grand Canal.

on one. Gondoliers are tightly regulated in the city and their fees are set at Euro 71 for 50 minutes and Euro 90 for 50 minutes at night. Many gondoliers will negotiate a slight discount for a 20–30-minute tour. Set the price before getting in the boat and defray the cost by going in a group.

If you want a short ride in a gondola but don't want to break the bank doing so, jump in a *traghetto*, the two-man gondolas that ferry people across the Grand Canal at six different points (look for the traghetto signs). A traghetto costs only Euro 0.40 and you are supposed to travel in it the way the locals do, standing up. Every gondolier licensed by the city is obliged to row a traghetto for a specified length of time each year.

Holidays and Festivals

Carnival is the granddaddy of all Venetian festivals and takes place during the ten days leading up to Lent. This is the highest of high seasons for Venice when hotel prices are at their peak. Book well in advance if you plan to be in Venice for Carnival. The Feast of La Sensa, or Ascension Day, is the modern recreation of the annual Doge's Marriage to the Sea. It happens every May on the Sunday after Ascension Day (in the Catholic calendar). While the ceremony is lacklustre to say the very least, of real interest is the gondola race that follows. In the same vein is the Historical Regatta, which is held every year on the first Sunday in September. It is a grand sight as period boats are rowed by Venetians in historic costume.

Lastly, there are two festivals that commemorate the end of historic plague outbreaks. The Feast of the Redeemer takes place on the third Sunday of July and is punctuated with a procession across the Giudecca Canal from the Zattere to Palladio's Church of Il Redentore over a pontoon bridge. Fireworks follow the procession and continue into the night. The Feast of Health (*Festa della Salute*) happens every year on 21 November and ends with a procession across a pontoon bridge from the *sestiere*, or district, of San Marco to the church of Santa Maria della Salute on the other side of the Grand Canal.

Discount Opportunities

Visitors planning to be in the city for more than a day or two should think about investing in a VENICECard. Available in one-, three- and seven-day varieties, these cards allow unlimited access to public transportation, access to public toilets and free admission to the city's museums. For more information, go to www.venicecard.com. Highly recommended.

Actv, the authority running the vaporetti public transportation system, sells 24-hour and 72-hour passes at their ticket booths in front of each stop.

Also of great value is the Chorus Pass, which is valid for one year and allows you to visit fifteen Venetian churches. You can visit each church once. Each of these churches charges Euro 2 for entrance but the Chorus Pass costs only Euro 8 (Euro 5 with a VENICECard). You can buy a Chorus Pass at any of the participating churches and all the funds go towards the restoration and maintenance of the buildings. Check out www.chorusvenezia.org/english/home_eng.htm for more information. Youths and students should consider getting an International Student Card, which offers discounts at some museums. Check out www. isiccard.com for more information.

Safety

Venice is probably the safest city in Italy and the local police do a great job of ensuring the safety of the 15 million visitors the city sees every year.

Venice for the Disabled

There is no other way to put it, Venice is a difficult place for the disabled traveller. Difficult but not impossible. Venice has recently installed wheelchair lifts on a handful of the city's bridges, giving some access. It is also possible for wheelchair-bound travellers to use the larger Vaporetti, such as those that service the Grand Canal, but even then you might be dependent on the boat crew to help you overcome the 15–30-centimetre (6–12-inch) height difference between the boat and the dock depending on the level of the water. The city of Venice does provide a map of accessible routes for the disabled on its website (http://english.comune.venezia.it/mappe/disabili/piantina_eng.asp).

A rule of thumb should be to view the canals as the barriers (because almost all of the canals are crossed via a step bridge) and the vaporetto stops as entrée points. Bearing this in mind, there is a surprisingly large part of the city that can be seen including St. Mark's Square, the Basilica, the Doge's Palace (which has a lift, ask at the front desk) and the Gallerie dell'Accademia.

Key for Cannaregio

1. Antico Doge
2. Bottega del Tintoretto
3. Ca d'Oro
4. Casino
5. Church of Madonna dell'Orto
6. Church of San Geremia
7. Church of Santa Maria Assunta
8. Church of Santi Apostoli
9. Fiaschetteria Toscana Salizzada
10. Gam Gam
11. Ghetto Vecchio

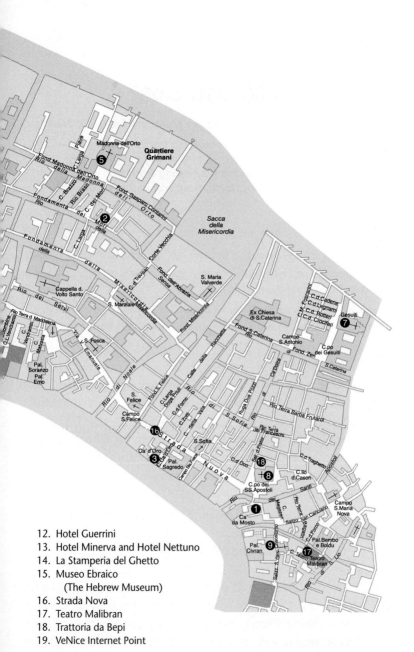

12. Hotel Guerrini
13. Hotel Minerva and Hotel Nettuno
14. La Stamperia del Ghetto
15. Museo Ebraico
    (The Hebrew Museum)
16. Strada Nova
17. Teatro Malibran
18. Trattoria da Bepi
19. VeNice Internet Point

A Million Lies?

Vestiges of Marco Polo's house, Teatro Malibran, Campiello Malibran

*Two merchant brothers make a daring trip into unexplored Asia
to meet the great Khan. After returning to Venice, they
make a second trip, this time taking a son who would
become the most famous explorer in the world.*

Venice was in a geographic position to succeed in medieval trade. Situated at the north end of the Adriatic, close to central Europe and open to the Mediterranean, the Middle East and North Africa, it stood at the crossroads of many major trade routes. Many Venetian families struck out to the East forgoing danger and hardship to bring back precious goods for profit, but none gained more success or fame than the Polo family.

The Polos were a well-established merchant family who moved to Venice from the nearby Dalmatian coast. Two Polo brothers, Matteo and Niccolo, operated a trading business between Venice and Constantinople but liquidated their holdings in the Byzantine capital and struck out for greater profits in central Asia, Niccolo leaving his wife and young son Marco behind in Venice. It was a venture that changed the world.

In the ancient city of Bukhara, the Polo brothers met an ambassador from the court of Mongolian ruler Kublai Khan who invited them to join him on his return to Asia. The Polos accepted and travelled all the way to Beijing, where they met the Great Khan in 1266. Kublai Khan was fascinated with the lands and peoples beyond his empire and hosted the Polo brothers for several years. When the Polos set their date to return home, Kublai Khan presented them with a golden tablet, which served as an empire-wide travel pass. About 30 centimetres (1 foot) long and 7 cm (3 inches) wide, it was inscribed with the Khan's will that the travellers presenting it should be afforded anything necessary for a safe passage. After nearly a decade of trade and adventure in the East, Niccolo, with his brother at his side, returned to his home city to find his wife had passed away and his son Marco almost a man.

After spending two years back in Venice, the brothers once again set out for China, this time taking Marco, aged 17, with them. It took four years for the three Polos to return to China in a trip that took them through Persia, Afghanistan and over the Himalayas along the Silk Road. The Polos presented the Khan with many gifts from the West and were again well received.

It seems that the Great Khan took a keen interest in young Marco. Marco, an accomplished linguist, was fascinated with this new land and took every opportunity to study the Khan's empire. While the older Polos picked up their trade, Kublai Khan put Marco's interest to good use by appointing him to head special missions to various parts of his empire such as India, Burma, Siam and Siberia. Marco took the golden tablet with him in the travels that would make him famous.

Marco remained in the service of Kublai Khan for 17 years, during which time Niccolo and Matteo amassed a sizeable fortune in jewels. With the Khan, now in his seventies, in questionable health, the Polos set a date to return again to Venice with their wealth. Marco retained the tablet with which all three gained safe passage out of Asia.

The story of the Polos' return to their home in Venice is likened to Homeric legend. Still dressed in their tattered Tartar clothing, they were received nearly two decades later as beggars in their own home. Unrecognisable to their Venetian brethren, the grubby three hosted a sumptuous banquet for their extended family. During the banquet, Niccolo, Matteo and Marco each donned a series of spectacular Asian garments for each course. After finally putting their dirty travel clothes back on, they linked arms before slitting open the seams and lining of their clothes, out of which poured a cascade of precious gems. Following this spectacle, the Polo family recognised their long-lost relatives.

The return of the Polos in 1295 caused quite a stir in Venice and Marco regaled the numerous callers at the family's home, the Ca' Polo, with his incredible tales of China, the Mongol horde and Kublai Khan's excesses, including his millions of subjects, his millions of soldiers, his millions of horses and so on. In a short time, Venetian society grew weary of these outlandish tales and Marco soon gained the mocking nickname of Marco Milione, or Marco Millions. Understandably, he became increasingly reluctant to divulge further tales of his adventures in Asia. It is highly likely that Marco Polo would have faded into obscurity had it not been for the next series of events in his life.

Three years after returning to Venice, as weary of Venetian society as it was of his perceived fables, Marco answered the call of duty and commanded a galley in the war against Genoa. He was captured in a battle and spent a year in a Genoese prison. While in prison, Marco shared a cell with a man named Rustichello, a writer of romances. In order to pass the time, Marco regaled the writer with the details from his travels, which Rustichello put to paper. Both men were released in 1299. Marco returned to Venice and Rustichello published Polo's stories in a book titled *The Travels of Marco Polo*. The book was an immediate success and was one of the most popular books of the medieval age in Europe. Yet Italy and the rest of Europe gave his account no more respect than his Venetian counterparts and newer editions of the book were published under the title of *Il Milione*, or *The Million Lies*.

Marco Polo, famous in our time, was widely discredited in his own. He lived in the family home in Venice into old age, reluctant to his final days to discuss his travels. On his deathbed, his friends and family beseeched him to recant his account of the Khan and his travels for the honour of the family to which he replied, "I have only told the half of what I saw!"

Upon his death, some thirty years after his return from Asia, his family discovered a cache of exotic cloths, silks and treasures in quantities exactly as he had described in his tales to Rustichello. With these they also discovered a golden tablet, measuring 30 cm by 7 cm and covered in Chinese glyphs.

Vindication

History has been much kinder to Polo than his contemporaries, who regarded his tales as mere fable. European travellers in the 18th century corroborated many of his accounts some 500 years before.

This plaque commemorates where Marco Polo lived upon his return to Venice. Marco Polo's house, the Ca' Polo, stood on the current location of the Teatro Malibran, where some architectural vestiges remain.

The First Ghetto

Ghetto Vecchio

*In the Middle Ages, Venice is the first city to force Jews
into a segregated enclave and its name for this first community
was to live in infamy.*

In the words of noted Jewish author and activist Elie Wiesel in *The Ghetto of Venice*: "The average tourist goes to Venice to visit the Rialto or the Lido, but Jews go there to see the ghetto. This is because, of all the medieval ghettos, the one in Venice is the most famous." The Venetian ghetto is also the first instance in Europe where Jews were segregated into a separate enclave, a convention that would live on for nearly 500 years.

Located at the crossroads of Europe, the Near East and the Ottoman Empire, Venice has been a melting pot since its founding as a city in the 400s. Since then, sailors, soldiers, merchants, pilgrims and refugees have combined to create a multicultural mix. While some historians claim that Jews have lived in Venice since the 11th century, it is certain that they lived and operated businesses on the island by the 14th century, as the terms of their tenure and trade were dictated by the Senate in a decree called a *condotto*. The first condotto limited Jews to selling second-hand clothing and jewellery but prevented them from manufacturing or selling new items that might have impacted the traditional Venetian (and Catholic) guilds. They were allowed to loan money at set rates and to live in the city. By 1397, the condotto had expired and all Jews were ordered to leave the city. Most retired to nearby Mestre on the mainland. Five years later, the restrictions were lifted, but with conditions. Jews were not allowed to stay in Venice for more than fifteen consecutive days and they could only stay once every four months. They were also required to wear circular yellow badges so that they could be easily recognised.

For the next 100 years, the Jews of Venice struggled to gain a permanent foothold on the island. Condottos expired, terms were renegotiated and then they expired again. By the 15th century, Venetians viewed Jews with emotions ranging from suspicion to contempt (on religious grounds) but, at the same time, the Doge and Senate were also warming to their usefulness. By obliging the Jews to loan money at below market rates of interest (these were fixed in the terms of the condotto) in exchange for permission to live in the city, the republic found much needed financing for the development of trade and for war.

The 1508 war waged against Venice by the League of Cambrai, an alliance formed by Pope Julius II of Rome, Holy Roman Emperor Maximilian I, King Louis XII of France and King Ferdinand II of Spain, put tremendous strain on the republic. In time, Venice lost most of its mainland territories. With its armies in retreat and refugees (many of them Jews) approaching the island, Venice achieved an ingenious and pragmatic solution. In consideration of loans, taxes and permits sold to Jews that enabled them to open shops, the Jews were allowed to live in the lagoon provided that they lived in a separate neighbourhood. The only remaining issue was where to put them.

At first, the islands of Murano and Giudecca were suggested but these proposals were rejected by both sides. The Senate rejected them on the grounds that the Jews would require boats to travel to Venice and that their comings and goings would be too difficult to police. Jewish leaders rejected the proposed locations because they were unprotected and malarial. In 1516, a compromise was reached. It was agreed that Jewish businessmen and refugees would live in an isolated area of Cannaregio that had been used as a foundry, or *geto* in Italian. The area was accessible only by a single bridge that could be guarded. On 29th March, the Senate announced:

"The Jews must all live together in the Corte de Case, which are in the Geto near San Girolamo; and in order to prevent their roaming about at night: Let there be built two gates on the side of the old geto

SOTOPORTEGO
DE GHETO NOVO

PAROCHIA
S . ALVISE

PONTE
DE GHETONOVO

This wooden bridge, Ponte de Gheto Novo, leads to the world's first Jewish ghetto. Not only were the Jews confined to their own small quarter of the city once the ghetto was established, they were also forced to pay for the four guards who kept nightly watch at the gates to their quarter. In addition, they had to pay for the two boats that patrolled the surrounding canals.

where there is a little bridge, that is each of two said places, which gates shall be opened in the morning at the sound of the Marangona (the morning bell from St. Mark's), and shall be closed at midnight by four Christian guards appointed and paid by the Jews at the rate deemed suitable by Our Cabinet."

And with this simple decree, the first Jewish ghetto was born.

The Origin of the Word "Ghetto"

The area designated for the first permanent Jewish settlement in Venice was known as the *geto* because it was the site of the city's foundries. The Venetian verb for smelting metal was *gettare* and, consequently, the noun for "foundry" became *geto*. The spelling and pronunciation of geto gradually evolved to our modern-day word "ghetto".

The ghetto was a mixed blessing for the Jews of Venice. While confining the Jews to their own quarter of the city enabled the Venetians to effectively demonstrate the inferiority of Jews (a common view in medieval and Renaissance Christian Europe), the ghetto also acted as a virtual fortress, providing the fledgling community with a refuge from violence or looting. These threats were quite real. The decree allowing Jews to live in Venice was not widely welcomed by the populace and firebrand Franciscans sermonised that God would punish the city if Jews were admitted.

A Fortress of Culture

The forced segregation of the Venetian Jews set an ugly racial precedent that echoes to our modern day but the ghetto also served to protect the Jewish culture in Venice by keeping it distinct from the rest of the city. This culture is best appreciated in the Jewish Museum and in the Scuola Grande Spagnola and Scuola Grande Tedesca, both functioning synagogues.

Over the next 100 years, the rights of and restrictions on Venetian Jews waxed and waned in direct proportion to the strength of the Venetian Inquisition or to the amount of money they could be compelled to lend in times of state emergency such as plague or war. Jews were mandated to wear a yellow armband or yellow hat while conducting business or venturing beyond the confines of the ghetto (during the day only). They were made to swear Christian oaths and many Jews attended Catholic churches outside of the ghetto under less than zealous pretences in order to avoid the attention of the Inquisition.

Eventually Venice's attitude of ambivalent tolerance prevailed and the Jews, with their financial and trade acumen, were integrated into the city commercially, if not civically.

We Can Only Go Up from Here

Due to the restricted size of the Jewish ghetto and the growth of the Jewish community, the residents had nowhere to go but up. Some buildings in the ghetto are six, seven or even eight storeys tall, a height unheard of in other parts of Venice.

The Jewish ghetto was expanded in 1541 and again in 1633 to the size it is today. Although the gates of the Venetian ghetto were torn down in 1797, the community continued on in relative isolation.

Each year, a large menorah is erected in the Campo di Ghetto Nuovo to celebrate the Jewish festival of Hanukkah.

INSIDER'S TIPS

Church of San Geremia Located at the end of the Lista di Spanga, this church contains a nice painting by Palma the Younger but its real attraction is the 4th-century corpse of Saint Lucy (Santa Lucia) who was martyred in Sicily. Her body was brought to Venice from Constantinople in 1204. You can see her body in a glass coffin near the back of the church. Free. Open 8am–noon, 3.30pm–6pm Monday to Saturday, 9am–noon, 5.30pm–6.30pm Sunday. Campo San Geremia.

Ghetto Vecchio The Hebrew Museum (Museo Ebraico) in the ghetto conducts tours in English every hour. The tour explains the history of the Jews in the lagoon and allows access into some of the city's historic synagogues. Admission Euro 3, Euro 8 (with guided tour). Open 10.30am–3.30pm Monday to Friday, 10.30am–4.30pm Sunday (open later in summer). Closed Saturday. Campo di Ghetto Nuovo. Tel: 041 715359. Website: www.jewishvenice.org

Church of Madonna dell'Orto This large Gothic church at the far north of the island boasts a treasure of works by Tintoretto, who lived nearby and is buried in the church (his tomb is on the right aisle). Of interest too are the statues of all twelve apostles decorating the façade, including a very rare depiction of Judas Iscariot. Euro 2 or Chorus Pass. Open 10am–5pm Monday to Saturday, 1pm–5pm Sunday. Campo Madonna dell' Orto.

Ca d'Oro The legendary House of Gold, this palazzo was once the most opulent in the city with a marble façade decorated with gold leaf. The gold leaf is gone today but the palazzo has recently been restored. The entrance fee also allows entry into the Ca d'Oro's art collection which contains two Carpaccios, a Titian and a Tintoretto. Euro 5. Open 8.15am–2pm Monday, 8.15am–7.15pm Tuesday to Sunday. Calle di Ca d'Oro. Website: www.cadoro.org/

Church of Santa Maria Assunta Located near the vaporetti stops at the Fondamenta Nuove, this out-of-the-way Jesuit church is a real gem. The artworks inside include a Titian and many by Palma the Younger (especially the sacristy to the left of the altar), but the real draw here is the marble inlaid interior. Free. Open daily 10am–noon, 4pm–6pm. Campo dei Gesuiti.

Church of Santi Apostoli Take a break from shopping on the Strada Nova to check out this humble church. It has one of the highest campaniles in the city. It also hosts the lovely *Manna from Heaven* by Veronese and a Tiepolo. Free. Open daily 8am–noon, 5pm–7pm. Campo dei Santi Apostoli (end of the Strada Nova).

Casino One of the few options for late nightlife in Venice, the Casino occupies the Palazzo Vendramin Calergi. It is worth a visit just to see Venice's wealthy routinely turn out to test their luck. Try your own, too. A bit stuffy with a dress code. Jackets required for men (provided at the cloakroom if you don't have one). Euro 10 entry fee (you will be given a chip worth Euro 10 with which to gamble as a rebate). Open daily 4pm–2.30am. Corte Rizzo. Website: www.casinovenezia.it

Antico Doge This quaint little three-star hotel is situated inside the old Palazzo del Doge Falier, once home to the disgraced and eventually beheaded Doge Marin Falier. Doubles with bath Euro 130–225. South end of Campo dei Santi Apostoli. Tel: 041 2411570. Website: www.anticodoge.com

Hotel Minerva and Hotel Nettuno These two hotels have just over 30 rooms combined. Very good quality for a one-star hotel. Some rooms have baths, some do not. Singles without bath Euro 50–63, doubles without bath Euro 61–87, triples without bath Euro 80–119. Singles with bath Euro 58–71, doubles with bath Euro 92–118, triples with bath Euro 114–153. 230 Lista di Spagna. Tel: 041 715968. Website: http://minervaenettuno.it

Hotel Guerrini Just down from the Minerva and Nettuno, the Guerrini boasts 30 rooms. Singles without bath Euro 60 and doubles without bath Euro 90. Singles with bath Euro 85 and doubles with bath Euro 120–150. Triples are Euro 170 and rare quads are a deal at Euro 180. 265 Lista di Spagna. Tel: 041 715333. Website: www.hotelguerrini.it

Gam Gam A kosher restaurant just at the edge of the Ghetto Vecchio. A wide variety of offerings. Fondamenta di Cannaregio. Tel: 041 715284.

Trattoria da Bepi Another great local eatery with seafood and vegetarian delights. The owner, Loris, makes you feel right at home.

Menus in Italian and English. Campo dei Santi Apostoli. Tel: 041 5285031

Fiaschetteria Toscana This unassuming restaurant is actually one of the best in the city. Great seafood and a stellar wine list. Menus in many languages. Reservations required. Salizzada San Giovanni Grisostomo. Tel: 041 5285281.

VeNice Internet Point A good internet café with many terminals. Euro 2.50 for 15 minutes. Lista di Spanga. Tel: 041 716185. Website: www.ve-nice.com

La Stamperia del Ghetto A great little art store featuring works from noted Italian Jews. Calle di Ghetto Vecchio. Tel: 041/2750200.

Bottega del Tintoretto Another *Insider's* first. This is not a shop so much as it is a school, an art school. This studio was once the workshop of Jacopo Robusti, better known as Tintoretto. Today, it is a working art studio and an art school headed by master artist Roberto Mazzetto. Topics include figurative drawing, painting and lithography. Private lessons cost Euro 15 per hour. Group lessons cost Euro 30 (for 4 hours). This is a unique opportunity to study art in a studio of historical significance. 3400 Fondamenta dei Mori. Tel: 041 722081. Website: www.tintorettovenezia.it (mainly in Italian, as are the classes but Roberto is patient and accommodating).

Paticceria Puppa A great pastry shop and quick café located near the Fondamenta Nova. Calle Stella.

Strada Nuova Along with the San Polo side of the Rialto, this is where the Venetians go to shop. This busy thoroughfare has a wide variety of offerings for a fraction of the price of the shops between San Marco and the Rialto.

Short Walk

Starting Point—Stazione Santa Lucia. From here, walk along the Fondamenta Santa Lucia towards Chiesa degli Scalzi on the same side of the canal (don't cross the bridge). Keep walking straight as the street turns into Rio Terrà Lista di Spanga. This will lead you to the Campo San Geremia and its church, San Geremia. Inside the church, you will find an interesting sight—the body of a saint, Saint Lucy to be exact. You can pass by and see her in a glass sarcophagus at the back of the church. Exit the campo along Salizz. San Geremia.
Cross the bridge (Ponte delle Guglie) and follow Rio Terrà San Leonardo until it forks. Take the left fork (Rio Terrà

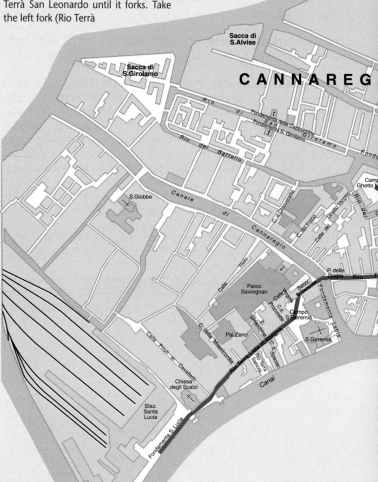

Farsetti). Turn left onto Calle Nuove, which becomes Calle Selle and then Calle Farnese before leading you to Campo Ghetto Nuovo, the heart of the Jewish ghetto. Retrace your steps back to the Rio Terrà Farsetti and follow it across the canal to the Fondamenta degli Ormesini. You are now in a distinctly Venetian neighbourhood. Go right on the Fondamenta degli Ormesini. Continue along the street, then turn left onto C. d. Forno and cross the canal. Next, turn onto the Fondamenta dei Mori until you reach C. dei Mori. Follow this until you find yourself at the foot of the huge church of Madonna dell'Orto. Go inside to see a handful of Tintoretto's artworks and his tomb. Then follow the Fondamenta Gasparo Contarini to its end and cross the canal onto Corte Vecchia. Don't cross the next bridge. Instead, turn left onto the Fondamenta dell'Abbazia and follow it to the end before crossing the bridge over to the Fondamenta Misericordia. Follow the fondamenta to the end, cross over the bridge and take the sottoportegio over to the Fondamenta San Felice. Go straight until you reach the Campo San Felice. Then turn left onto the Strada Nuova. Walk along this promenade until you reach the Campo dei Santi Apostoli.

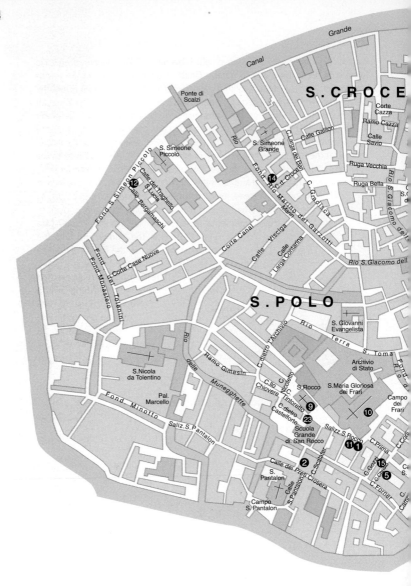

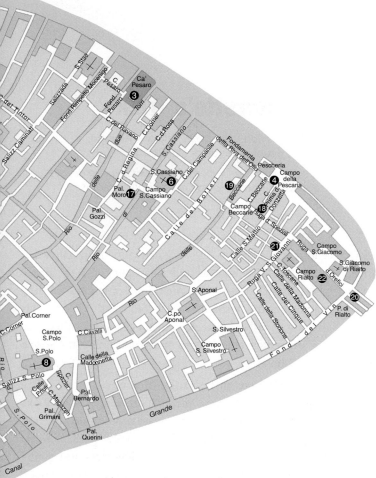

Key for Santa Croce and San Polo

1. Atelier Marega
2. Bucintoro
3. Ca' Pesaro
4. Campo della Pescheria
5. CasanovaMask
6. Church of San Cassiano
7. Church of San Giacomo dell'Orio
8. Church of San Polo
9. Church of San Rocco
10. Church of Santa Maria Gloriosa dei Frari
11. Forma
12. Hotel Airone
13. Hotel Alex
14. Hotel Basilea
15. La Bottega dei Mascareri
16. La Zucca
17. Nona Risorto
18. Peoceto Risorto
19. Poste Vecie
20. Rialto Bridge
21. Ruga Vecchia
22. Sacro e Profano
23. Scuola Grande di San Rocco
24. Trattoria Captain Uncino

Tintoretto's Trick

The Glorification of St. Roch, Sala dell'Albergo,
Scuola Grande di San Rocco

*A master painter covets an important commission and devises
a clever trick, at the expense of his rivals, to win it.*

The 16th century was a Golden Age for gifted painters in Italy when artists like Michelangelo, Raphael and Titian put brush to canvas. Their works filled churches as well as the homes of families wealthy enough to commission the best artists they could find. Yet even this proved to be a limited market for so many talents. In Venice, there was another market for painters who worked on a grand scale—the Scuole Grandi, or Grand Schools.

The Scuole Grandi were an institution unique to Venice. They began in the 13th century as loose confederations of public penitents who practised self-flagellation in times of disease or strife. Very quickly, these organisations changed into benevolent confraternities, or social brotherhoods, dedicated to performing charitable acts and giving donations to the city, including, for example, giving ducats to the poor, setting aside dowries for impoverished unmarried girls and providing for troops.

The six largest scuole became very prestigious organisations that attracted a wide membership from the wealthy merchant and professional classes, who looked to improve their own social status. The expensive membership dues to these scuole allowed for many charitable deeds, but also for much more artistic ostentation. The largest, richest and, coincidentally, the most ostentatious of these six scuole was the Scuola Grande di San Rocco.

The entrance to the magnificent Scuola Grande di San Rocco.

The construction of the Scuola Grande di San Rocco began in 1515 and was completed in 1560. Four years later, the scuola was ready for its first artworks. Therefore, it held a competition to see which artist would execute the all-important inaugural painting. The artists of the city knew the commission would be an important one, as it would no doubt lead to subsequent orders to provide paintings for the large building. The scuola requested the selected artists to submit sketches and outlines for the subject of the initial work—*The Glorification of St. Roch*—which was to be placed in the centre of the ceiling of the grand Sala dell'Albergo. The four artists invited to compete were Francesco Salviati, Taddeo Zuccari, Paolo Veronese and Jacopo Robusti, also known as Tintoretto.

The Dyer's Son

Jacopo Robusti took the widely known nickname Tintoretto because he was the son of a fabric dyer.

By 1564, Tintoretto had already enjoyed nearly two decades of success in his Cannaregio workshop and was already an established force in the northern Italian painting scene. He had watched the Scuola Grande di San Rocco being constructed his whole life and he desperately wanted to leave his mark on the building. His first attempt at ingratiating himself with the leaders of the scuola came in 1549 when he completed a commission for the scuola for the adjacent Church of San Rocco. The painting, *St. Roch Healing the Plague Stricken*, was intended as a gift that would secure his entry into the prestigious fraternity. The scuola accepted the painting but his request for admission was rejected on the advice of his former master turned bitter rival and one-time member of the scuola, Titian. Undeterred, Tintoretto, now with many friends inside the scuola, saw his opportunity with the invitation to enter the competition.

In the few weeks allocated to complete the sketches, Tintoretto worked alone feverishly in his studio creating a completed masterwork. The night before the contest, the artist carried his oval masterpiece to the scuola, where a few friends secretly installed the painting in position on the ceiling of the Sala dell'Albergo and covered it with a cloth. The next day, all four artists arrived, one curiously not carrying any designs. In turn, Salviati, Zuccari and Veronese displayed and explained their small, lifeless black-on-white sketches. When it came to Tintoretto's turn, he walked over to the wall and pulled on a rope attached to the cloth covering his masterpiece. The cloth fell to the floor, along with the hopes of the three other artists. They knew they had been beaten. The elders of the scuola knew it too and they granted the already completed commission to Tintoretto.

The Sala dell'Albergo in the Scuola Grande di San Rocco contains a number of striking paintings including The Glorification of St. Roch *in the centre of the ceiling.*

Salviati, Zuccari and Veronese protested bitterly, stating that the contest was for designs only and not for completed works, to which Tintoretto replied that that was his method of making designs and he did not know how to proceed in any other manner. His rivals continued to complain to the elders of the scuola so, in the end, Tintoretto donated the work in order to silence them. The painting has not been moved since.

Victorious, Tintoretto now had his foot in the door of the Scuola Grande di San Rocco and he was determined to push all the way in. The following year, his membership application into the scuola was approved by an overwhelming majority. Not only that, his initial commission led to further commissions to decorate the entire Sala dell'Albergo, including his colossal masterwork *The Crucifixion*.

The Plague Saint

St. Roch (San Rocco) is the patron saint of plague victims. Given the plague outbreaks of the era, a flood of donations poured into the church and scuola of San Rocco in the hope of deliverance from plague outbreaks in the city in the 16th century. Tintoretto may have felt great reverence for St. Roch as his entire family was spared during the plague of 1575 to 1577, which claimed one in every four Venetians, including his rival Titian.

For the remainder of his life, Tintoretto dedicated himself largely to the decoration of the Scuola Grande di San Rocco. He originally offered to provide subsequent paintings for the scuola at a greatly discounted fee, which again drew the ire of his rivals. Then, in 1575, Tintoretto put forth an interesting offer to the directors of the scuola. He offered to execute paintings on a full-time basis for the entire building until the end of his days in return for a small flat fee of 100 ducats per year. The directors accepted the artist's offer and, as a result, over the next 19 years, the scuola became almost an entire Tintoretto installation, consisting of over 50 individual works.

School's Out Forever

The unique social institutions of the Scuole Grandi, like many things associated with the long-lived Venetian republic, came to an end with the arrival of Napoleon

40   Insider's VENICE

in 1797. Fortunately, however, the Scuola Grande di San Rocco has survived to the present day remarkably intact. Venice's other Scuole Grandi were not so lucky. The Scuola Grande di San Marco was converted into a hospital. The Scuola Grande di Maria della Misericordia became a sports club and the Scuola Grande di Maria della Carita was converted into the lovely Gallerie dell'Accademia.

Today, no trip to Venice is complete without visiting the Scuola Grande di San Rocco to admire Tintoretto's works. The 19th-century traveller and author John Ruskin put it best when he called the scuola "one of the three most precious buildings in Italy", behind the Sistine Chapel in Rome and the Campo Santo in Pisa.

Tintoretto's Modern Studio

Tintoretto's studio was on the ground floor of his home on the Fondamenta dei Mori in Cannaregio. His home and, more importantly, his studio still stand today thanks to the ongoing efforts of modern master artist Roberto Mazzetto. Mazzetto and company run a printmaking laboratory and teach classes in printmaking, fresco, watercolour, mosaic and sculpture.

What News on the Rialto?

Rialto Bridge

After several attempts, Venice's oldest neighbourhood finally gets a bridge built to last.

The banks of the Grand Canal near the Rialto Bridge are some of the highest, most stable ground on the island. They are also the site of the oldest settlements of Venice, dating back to the 9th century. Furthermore, the little church of San Giacomo di Rialto at the base of the western end of the bridge is the oldest surviving church in the city. Home to the current city market, the Rialto neighbourhood has always been the city's centre for commerce. William Shakespeare immortalised this neighbourhood's unique mix of trade, money lending and rumour in *The Merchant of Venice* when the play's main character, Shylock, the rich Jewish money lender, uttered the famous line, "What news on the Rialto?"

One of the first problems that early merchants of Venice had to resolve was how to link both parts of this striving neighbourhood together. The answer, of course, was a bridge. There has been a bridge of one sort or another at the Rialto since the 1100s and, up until 1854, the Rialto Bridge (in its many incarnations) was the only way in which to cross the Grand Canal on foot. Noted Venetian engineer Nicolo Barattieri (the man who erected both the columns in St. Mark's Square) constructed the first recorded Rialto Bridge in 1181. It was a pontoon-type bridge consisting of a simple walkway that was laid down over a series of connected boats across the canal. Around 1255, a permanent wooden bridge was constructed. This bridge, however, was badly damaged by Bajamonte Tiepolo during his escape from a disastrous coup attempt in 1310. Repairs were made and the bridge was reopened. The wooden bridge, interesting in its drawbridge design as seen in the period painting *Miracle of the True Cross* by Carpaccio (now in the Gallerie dell'Accademia), eventually proved insufficient; it collapsed in 1444 under the weight of gathered onlookers to the wedding procession of the Marquis of Ferrara. Another wooden bridge was erected, this one lined with small shops, but it too collapsed into the Grand Canal in 1524. A more durable crossing was needed.

Carpaccio's vibrant Miracle of the True Cross *centres on the view of the Rialto Bridge and the banks on either side of the Grand Canal in Renaissance Venice.*

The Senate made a decision to construct a stone bridge over the canal in 1524 and, in 1557, an open competition was announced for designs from some of Italy's finest architects. In a process fraught with delays spanning decades, designs were submitted and rejected from famous and not-so-famous talents. Sansovino, Palladio, Michelangelo, Vignola, Scamozzi, Lazzari, Marastoni and others submitted a wide variety of designs, including single, three- and five-arch span designs, Romanesque colonnaded neoclassical works and one design that allowed for a six-storey building to be built atop a single span bridge. The Senate considered all of these designs but could not agree on which one to choose. In January 1588, realising that it was unlikely they would ever reach a consensus on the strong designs submitted by

Italy's best, the members of the Senate turned to an unlikely architect to build the new bridge.

Antonio da Ponte was already an accomplished, if not famous, Venetian architect in 1588, having designed and constructed the new prison opposite the Doge's Palace. He worked well with members of the Senate, was reliable and took instruction and artistic input with ease. These were the main factors why his single span design was accepted, following, of course, instructions from the Senate members, who had enjoyed the benefit of reviewing the best designs available. They commissioned his modified simple design to include two exterior walkways to afford unobstructed views of the Grand Canal and a central walkway to divide two rows of shops. Antonio da Ponte chose as his assistant his architect nephew Antonio Contino, who would later complete the famous Bridge of Sighs after his uncle's death.

What's in a Name?

One might say that Antonio da Ponte was predestined for the Rialto Bridge contract as his name translates to Antony of the Bridge. His name was to suit him well as an architect in Venice. He designed not only the Rialto Bridge but also the Bridge of Sighs, which connects the Doge's Palace to the prison, which he also designed and built.

Construction began with the removal of the badly dilapidated wooden bridge. Then long wooden pilings were driven deep down into the clay subsoil, 6000 for each side. The construction progressed quickly and without any problems—another da Ponte trademark. The bridge was opened in 1591 but its unique profile gained mixed reviews.

Englishman and noted Roman scholar Edward Gibbon described it as "a fine bridge spoilt by two rows of houses upon it". English traveller and author Fynes Moryson called it "the eighth miracle of the world". Regardless of opinion, the Rialto Bridge with its unique design has been elevated into the untouchable echelons of landmark structures. Like the Eiffel Tower, London Bridge or the Kremlin, the Rialto Bridge thrives now on its own personality, its own fame.

The Rialto Bridge is also known locally as la moneta, *which literally means "the coin". This nickname dates back to when a barge bridge was built across the Grand Canal in 1172. It was a crude bridge made of a number of walking planks laid over a series of tethered boats. The fee to cross the bridge was a single coin,* la moneta, *which was presumably cheaper than hiring a boat.*

The true genius in the design of the Rialto Bridge is its endless utility. At a height of 7.5 metres (24.6 feet) above water level, the single span allowed the tallest of the canal-going vessels of the day to pass while the balustraded exterior walkways afforded splendid views up and down the Grand Canal. For over four centuries, the bridge has been a haven for visitors. And only in Venice, where a one-time trading giant has had to trade on its fading beauty for revenue, could shops on a bridge seem so apropos.

Surviving Designs

It is interesting to think about the designs that could have been. Several models and paintings from the proposed designs still survive to this day, including Canaletto's painting of Palladio's interesting three-span design, which is housed in the Royal Collection in London, and Lazzari's classical single-span design, which can be found in the Museo Correr in Venice.

The Glories of Venice

Church of Santa Maria Gloriosa dei Frari, Campo dei Frari

Venice's largest church is host to a staggering collection of inspired works from local artists and is still home to three of them.

Situated deep in the San Polo *sestiere* stands the imposing Church of Santa Maria Gloriosa dei Frari, a large barn of a building constructed, in uncharacteristic Venetian fashion, almost entirely out of plain red bricks. This enormous edifice, at first glance, might look quite plain compared to its ornate neighbours—the church and adjoining scuola of San Rocco—but don't be fooled. The church's exterior might reflect the humble sensibilities of its Franciscan founders but the interior rivals the Museo Correr or the Gallerie dell'Accademia for its diversity of artworks. This church became such a mecca for artistic expression that it provided the final resting place for three giants of the Italian art world.

The founding of Santa Maria Gloriosa dei Frari, or the Frari for short, dates back to the first half of the 13th century when Doge Jacopo Tiepolo gave the republic's homeless Franciscans a small plot of land. The only problem was that the land had a lake on it. Never ones to shy away from hard work, the Franciscan monks drained the lake and shored up the site over the next five years, quickly erecting a small church thereafter. With two more small grants of land, the monks then had a plot large enough to accommodate a grander church, a campanile, a monastery and an adjoining campo. In 1338, however, the Franciscans decided to build a larger and grander church. After more than 100 years of construction, they had completed the enormous red-brick Frari that we see today.

The next order of business for the monks was to engage artists to fill the cavernous church with artworks and they did so with a diverse but generally tasteful approach. The first work was a dual choir of 124 hand-carved wooden stalls on either side of the apse. These works are amazingly preserved and show detail not equalled in any other piece of woodcarving in the city. Next, they commissioned a glorious altarpiece triptych from Giovanni Bellini. This altarpiece was moved to the far right-hand corner of the back wall after Titian painted his incomparable *The Assumption of the Virgin* for the Franciscans in 1518. Titian's masterwork dominates the central altar, with its mix of primal colours and radiant glory.

To complement these works, the Franciscans tapped the talents of Donatello, who contributed his stirring yet stark wooden sculpture of St. John the Baptist, located just right of the altar; Bartolomeo Vivarini, who contributed a triptych found in the Cappella Corner (Corner Chapel) at the far left of the back wall of the church; and even Jacopo Sansovino, who completed the marble statue of St. John the Baptist. Over the years, many other noted artists contributed to the pantheon of works housed in the Frari.

As lustrous as the Frari's decorations are, they pale in comparison to those buried there. The Church of Santa Maria Gloriosa dei Frari is the final resting place for three doges, a bishop, a famous military commander and one of the benefactors of the church. But the most famous of those interred in the Frari are its artists.

The first artist of note is the father of the opera, Claudio Monteverdi. Monteverdi was born in Cremona and began his music career as a choirboy in the local cathedral. He later went on to compose music under contract for the duke of nearby Mantua. When the music director for St. Mark's Basilica died in 1612, Monteverdi was encouraged to travel to Venice to compete for the vacant post. He won and held the coveted post of *maestro di cappella* of St. Mark's until his death in 1643. A plaque in the floor near the Cappella Corner marks his final resting place.

The second famous artist in the Frari is commemorated by a monument that cannot be missed (though some think it should).

Antonio Canova was born in nearby Possagno, the son of a stone cutter, in 1757. His talents as an artist were discovered when he supposedly carved a lion out of butter at a banquet table when he was seven. He subsequently became an apprentice to sculptor Guiseppe Bernardi, who moved his studio and Canova to Venice in 1568. Canova's career flourished in Venice and took him to Rome and Paris, where he worked for Napoleon and his family. Canova died in Venice in 1822, having designed the oddly out-of-place pyramidal tomb in the Frari as a monument to Titian, who, no doubt, would have recoiled at the thought. The tomb was completed by Canova's students, renamed for their master and dedicated to Canova in 1827.

While Canova is buried in his native Possagno, his heart is interred in an urn of porphyry inside the tomb designed by him in the Frari.

Canova's Tomb, by Canova

The sculptor's tomb is so out of place that even Canova himself might have rethought the idea of placing it in the Frari. In *The Stones of Venice*, author John Ruskin said of it: "...the Tomb of Canova, by Canova, cannot be missed; consummate in science, intolerable in affectation, ridiculous in conception, null and void to the uttermost in invention and feeling."

Canova's students, and the Franciscans too no doubt, let discretion reign when placing Canova in the tomb of his own design and beginning work anew on a monument for its originally intended honouree. Titian's monument is directly across the nave from Canova's. This enormous work was executed by Canova's pupils on what is reputed to be the exact spot where Titian was buried following his death in 1576. Titian died of the plague at the ripe age of 86. The fact that the master was allowed burial inside the church (it was usually unthinkable for a plague victim to be buried in any church) is testament to his esteem among the Franciscans.

Titian's tomb in the south aisle of the Frari faces Canova's large marble pyramid tomb.

The First Carnival

La Bottega dei Mascareri, Calle del Cristo 2919, San Polo

*For two weeks a year, Venice is awash in the colourful masks of Carnival
but the annual celebration is a shadow of what it once was.*

When people think of Venice, many think of its trademark gondolas
plying its canals or pigeons in St. Mark's Square, but those who
truly know the city think of the masks of Carnival. And there is no
better place in the city to get an idea of what Carnival is all about than
La Bottega dei Mascareri, the mask shop of Venice.

Carnival, or *Carnevale* in Italian, has been a Venetian tradition on and
off since the 12th century. This makes it the first Carnival celebration in
the world, predating those of Rio de Janeiro and New Orleans. While
most associate Carnival with Catholic pre-Lenten celebrations, it had
far different beginnings.

The tradition of Carnival, or rather the first event that evolved into
the modern Carnival festival, dates back to the 12th century. In 1162,
Ulrico, the patriarch of the nearby city of Aquileia, along with twelve
feudal lords from Carinzia and Friuli, attacked and drove the Venetians
out of the coastal city of Grado. The Venetian Doge at the time, Vitale
Michiel II, quickly counterattacked and captured Ulrico and the other
twelve men. He released the men, however, on the condition that they
sent one bull and twelve fattened pigs to Venice as proxy prisoners every
year on the day that the Venetians celebrated the victory.

A Bloody Mess

In its early days, the Carnival in Venice consisted of many cruel and bloody sports,
such as bullfighting, bull baiting (in which a tethered bull was tormented by dogs)

and a curious sport in which men shaved their heads and tried to bludgeon to death a white cat using only their bald heads. At one time, the festivities were concluded with the ritual slaughter of a bull.

The first mention of masks in Venice dates back to a decree in 1268 that forbade masqueraders from throwing eggs at Venetians not wearing masks on Shrove Tuesday. By the 1400s, the wearing of masks in association with Shrove Tuesday celebrations was well established.

The Carnival of Renaissance Venice was quite different from what a modern attendee would expect. The two-week celebration was marked by men competing in feats of strength, human pyramid building and wrestling. Vendors competed in wheelbarrow races and masked men strutted about on stilts, often stopping to loiter and speak with women sitting on their second-floor balconies. Venetians, both rich and poor, noble and common, attended lavish balls and paraded around the city in a contest to determine who had the best mask. The festivities were built upon and continued every day until the finale on Shrove Tuesday.

On the last day of the Carnival, revellers from all quarters of the city converged on St. Mark's Square to see a breathtaking feat of acrobatics that came to be known as the 'Flight of the Turk'. In the mid-1500s, a young Turkish acrobat delighted the crowd of masqueraders in St. Mark's by ascending to the top of the Campanile in the piazza via a tightrope tethered to the belfry at one end and a ship floating in the Grand Canal at the other. The feat so fascinated the assembled crowd that it became a Carnival tradition performed by subsequent acrobats and eventually specially trained workers from the nearby Arsenale naval shipyard. Many of the acrobats began wearing costume wings. Consequently, the annual flight was renamed the 'Flight of the Angel'. The acrobat concluded his descent by presenting a bouquet of flowers to the Doge. The Carnival then ended with masqueraders in the piazza singing, "It is going, it is going, the Carnival is going."

The two weeks of Carnival turned the city into a place of mystery and intrigue as vice abounded in complete anonymity. Nobles could mix with commoners, prostitutes with nuns, debtors with their lenders all incognito and all without repercussions come Ash Wednesday.

Each year, Venice comes alive during Carnival festivities when people wear elaborate costumes and masks.

Carnival became so wild in its early years, when it could commonly last from Christmas until mid summer, that a series of laws were enacted to restrict the festivities and to prevent further moral decline. Men were forbidden to enter convents dressed as women, gamblers were forbidden to wear masks in casinos for fear by lenders that current debtors might run up even higher losses, masqueraders were forbidden to enter churches and, in 1608, the Senate, in an attempt to limit the growing Carnival season, decreed it a crime to wear a mask outside of the traditional two-week Carnival period. The penalties were severe in typical Venetian fashion: two years in jail for men followed by 18 months chained to a galley oar while women who donned a mask beyond Shrove Tuesday were publicly whipped from St. Mark's Square all the way to the Rialto Bridge before being banned from the city for four years.

The fall of the republic in 1797 and subsequent Austrian occupation were bleak times for masqueraders as Carnival was often cancelled in protest. Furthermore, the event was not revived with the city's integration into a free Italy in 1886. Carnival was only reestablished in 1980 when a group of youths began masquerading in the two weeks before Lent.

Today, Carnival is an official festival complete with private masquerade balls for celebrities and local elites. Regular revellers dance the night away in St. Mark's Square. The thrilling Flight of the Angel, long a staple of Carnival, was reintroduced in the 1990s with a large wooden dove that descended from the Campanile. Since 2001, however, the flight has been enacted by a human performer.

INSIDER'S TIPS

Church of Santa Maria Gloriosa dei Frari Often simply referred to as the Frari, this church contains numerous exceptional works of art. Inside is one of Titian's most famous works, *The Assumption of the Virgin*. He was buried in the church, as was the celebrated sculptor Antonio Canova. Other important works include pieces by Sansovino, Donatello and Bellini. Euro 2.50 or Chorus Pass. Open 9am–6pm Monday to Saturday, 1pm–6pm Sunday. Campo dei Frari.

Scuola Grande di San Rocco This building, even more than the Church of Santa Maria dell'Orto, serves as a dazzling monument dedicated to Tintoretto as he decorated almost all of the interior. Take your time to soak everything in. Euro 5.50, reduced to Euro 4 with VENICECard. Open daily 9am–5.30pm March to November; 10am–4pm November to March (last entrance 30 minutes before closing). Campo San Rocco. Tel: 041 5234864. Website: www. scuolagrandesanrocco.it/

Church of San Rocco This church contains even more paintings by Tintoretto. Fumiani's ceiling painting is also nice. Fumiani made a living out of painting high ceilings in churches. His chosen profession killed him when he fell from the ceiling in the nearby Church of San Pantalon. Free. Open daily 7.30am–12.30pm, 4pm–6pm. Campo San Rocco. Tel: 041 5234864.

Church of San Polo Located in one of the quietest of Venice's native campos, this church deserves a visit to see its painting treasures. Inside you will find paintings by Tintoretto, Veronese, Palma the Younger and Tiepolo. Euro 2.50 or Chorus Pass. Open 10am–5pm Monday to Saturday, 1pm–5pm Sunday. Campo San Polo. Tel: 041 2750462.

Church of San Giacomo dell'Orio Pay a visit to this church to admire the altarpiece by Lorenzo Lotto as well as other works by Bassano and Veronese. Euro 2.50 or Chorus Pass. Open 10am–5pm Monday to Saturday, 1pm–5pm Sunday. Campo San Giacomo dell'Orio. Tel: 041 2750462.

Church of San Cassiano This unassuming church houses three works by Tintoretto. Free. Open daily 9am–noon, 5pm–7pm. Campo San Cassiano.

Rialto Bridge Most of the shops here are trinket traps but there are a few interesting shops on the bridge. Grand Canal.

Ca' Pesaro The Ca' Pesaro now houses the city's modern art museum. It boasts an interesting collection that nicely compliments the Peggy Guggenheim Collection. Euro 5.50, reduced to Euro 3 with VENICECard. Open 10am–5pm November–March; 10am–6pm April to October. Last entrance one hour before closing. Closed Monday. Fondamenta Pesaro. Tel: 041 5240695. Website: www.museiciviciv012eziani.it/main.asp?lin=EN

Poste Vecie Founded in 1500, the charming Poste Vecie (The Old Place) is billed as the oldest restaurant in Venice and with food this good, it is easy to figure out why. You will not find a more tender squid anywhere. Fantastic. Euro 10–20 per plate. Closed Tuesday. Rialto Pescheria. Tel: 041 721822. Website: www.postevecie.com

Peoceto Risorto A longtime favourite with Queen Elizabeth II, U.S. President Eisenhower and Hollywood royalty like Clark Gable and Joan Crawford. Euro 15–25 per plate. Closed Friday. Rialto Pescheria. Tel: 041 5225953.

Nona Risorto A great yet unpretentious place for pizza and pasta dishes. Good food at a good price. Euro 10 or less per plate. Open until midnight. Closed Wednesday. Just off Campo San Cassiano. Tel: 041 5241169.

La Zucca La Zucca (The Pumpkin) offers a wide selection of vegetarian dishes. Euro 10–15 per plate. Open 12.30pm–2.30pm, 7pm–10.30pm Monday to Saturday. Just north of Campo San Giacomo dell'Orio. Tel: 041 5241570. Website: www.lazucca.it

Trattoria Captain Uncino Although Captain Uncino (Captain Hook in English) may seem an unlikely eatery, it is a good restaurant with a strong wine list and an unbeatable cheese list. Euro 10–20 per plate. Campo San Giacomo dell'Orio. Tel: 041 721901.

Sacro e Profano Sacred and Profane, as the restaurant translates into English, is a true local *osteria*, or eatery. Handwritten menus (in Italian only) reflect what is fresh that day. With seating only for 14, it is advised to arrive early. Euro 10–20 per plate. Inside the Rialto Market. Tel: 041 5201931.

Hotel Alex Cheap, simple, clean and right next to the Frari. This one-star hotel offers doubles with bath for Euro 80–99 and singles with shared bath for Euro 35–46. Calle Rio Terra. Tel: 041 5231341.

Hotel Basilea Located in a quiet area near the Stazione Santa Lucia, the three-star Basilea is decorated in period Venetian style for a decent price. Singles with bath between Euro 70–140, doubles with bath between Euro 90–200, triples with bath between Euro 120–250 and even quads with bath between Euro 150–300. 817 Fondamenta Rio Marin. Tel: 041 718477. Website: www.hotelbasilea.com

Hotel Airone The two-star Airone offers good value for money with some rooms overlooking the Grand Canal. Singles with bath Euro 52–110, doubles with bath Euro 72–175, triples Euro 90–250. Fondamenta San Simone Piccolo. Tel: 041 5204991. Website: www.aironehotel.com

Ruga Vecchia San Giovanni All the shopping in the world is available here. Located near the Rialto Bridge, this is where Venetians shop for a fraction of the prices in shops near San Marco.

Campo della Pescheria While near the Rialto Bridge, a visit to the Pescheria is a must as is the Erberia. While there, check out the horsemeat butcher shop, a delicacy in parts of northern Italy and Switzerland.

Forma Normally, I would not include a fossil and insect shop but this one is cool and creepy. Definitely worth a quick stop. Campo San Rocco. Tel: 041 5231794.

Atelier Marega Right next door to Forma, this mask and costume shop rents costumes for Carnival. Campo San Rocco. Tel: 041 5221634. Website: www.marega.it

Bucintoro Yet another great pastry shop. Many local Venetian delicacies. Calle Scaletei.

CasanovaMask Stop in here to see how Carnival masks are made. 2210 Calle del Cristo. Tel: 041 5242739. Website: www.casanovamask.com

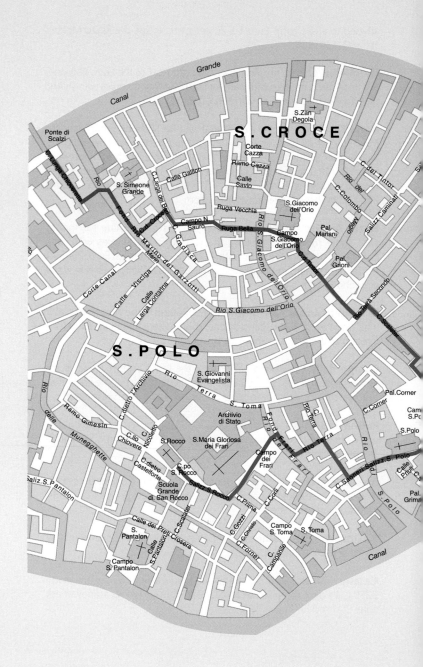

Grande

Canal

Ponte di
Scalzi

S. CROCE

S.Zan
Degola

Corte
Cazza

Ramo Cazza

S. Simeone
Grande

Calle Galfion

Calle
Savio

C. del Tintor

C. del

C. Colombo

Rio del

Megio

Salizz Caminati

Ruga Vecchia

S.Giacomo
dell'Orio

Pal.
Mariani

Fondamenta Minotto

Larga dei Bari

Campo N
Sauro

Rio Ter Marino del Garzotti

C. Gradisca

Ruga Bella

Rio S.Giacomo dell'Orio

Campo
S.Giacomo
dell'Orio

C. Colombo

Pal.
Grioni

Corte Canal

Calle — Visciga

Calle
Larga Contarina

Rio S.Giacomo dell'Orio

Rio Ter Secondo

C.Scaleter

S. POLO

Rio

Terra

S. Giovanni
Evangelista

Rio
delle

Ramo Gimesin

Munegghette

C. dietro l'Archivio

Rio

Terra

S. Toma

Archivio
di Stato

Rio Terra

Fond. dei Frari

Rio Terra

Pal.Corner

C.Corner

Cam
S.Po

Saliz.S. Pantalon

C.llo
Chiovere

C.
Nicoletto

S.Rocco

S.Maria Gloriosa
dei Frari

Campo
dei
Frari

C. Saoneri

Saliz.z. S. Polo

S.Polo

Pal.
Grima

C. dietro
Castelforte

C.po
S. Rocco

Saliz. S. Rocco

C. Corte

C.Prima

Calle
Priuli

S. POLO

Calle dei Preti Crosera

C.Scaleter

S.
Pantalon

Scuola
Grande
di San Rocco

Calle S. Pantalon

C.Gozzi

C.Ghitele

Campo
S. Toma

S. Toma

C.Forner

C.
Campanile

Canal

Campo
S. Pantalon

Short Walk

Starting Point—Ponte degli Scalzi. Follow Calle Lungo Chioverette and turn left onto Calle Bernami. Cross the Rio Marin onto the Fondamenta. Then turn left into C. d. Croce, which joins the Campo Nazario Sauro. Cross the campo to Ruga Bella. Then cross the canal and enter the lovely Campo San Giacomo dell'Orio. From this campo, take the Calle Tintor, cross the canal and follow the road until you reach the Rio Terrà Secondo. Turn right onto the Calle Scaleter, which crosses a canal and opens into Campo San Polo, one of the largest campos in Venice.

From Campo San Polo, take Saliz. San Polo out of the campo until it reaches Calle Saoneri. Veer right and head to the wide Rio Terra. Then turn left until you reach the Fondamenta Frari. Cross the bridge to enter the Campo dei Frari and visit the church. Follow the campo around the church to arrive at the Campo San Rocco, which contains both the scuola and the church of San Rocco.

From there, retrace your steps back to Campo San Polo. From the campo, take the Calle Madonnetta across the canal and go straight until you arrive in the Campo San Aponal. From Aponal, you have a choice of two routes: the scenic route and the shopping route. For the scenic route, turn right into Calle d. Uganegher. After you have reached Campo San Silvestro and its church, follow the traghetto sign to the Grand Canal. Once you reach the Grand Canal, turn left and follow the Fondamenta del Vin to the Rialto Bridge. For the shopping route, take Calle dell'Olio onto the Ruga Vecchia San Giovanni. Then turn left onto the Ruga dei Orefici. Finally, turn right and head to the Rialto Bridge.

Key for Dorsoduro and Giudecca

1. 65 Pizza
2. Aquarama
3. Ca della Corte
4. Café Blue
5. Calle dei Preti Crosera
6. Church of Il Redentore
7. Church of La Zitelle
8. Church of San Giorgio Maggiore
9. Church of San Sebastiano
10. Church of San Trovaso
11. Church of Santa Maria del Rosario
12. Church of Santa Maria della Salute
13. Gallerie dell'Accademia
14. Gobbetti
15. Hotel Pausania
16. Le Forcole
17. Loris Marazzi (Scultore di Madera)
18. Mondo Novo
19. Ostello Venezia
20. Peggy Guggenheim Collection
21. Squero di San Trovaso
22. Tonolo
23. Trattoria Osteria Venessiana
24. Vinus Venezia

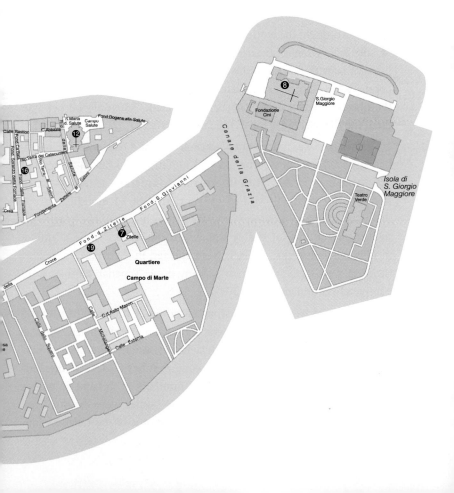

Death in Venice

Church of Santa Maria della Salute, Campo della Salute

The Senate of Venice takes a bold leap of faith in an attempt to break the grip of a plague epidemic, which would eventually kill one in three Venetians.

The sea brought the world and its riches to Venice: spices from India, silks from China and carpets from Asia Minor but, in 1630, the sea brought something else to the island—death. Death came in the form of rats (always a problem in waterborne Venice) or, to be more specific, the plague-infected fleas that the rats hosted. When all the rats had died, the diseased fleas turned to larger hosts.

The plague was nothing new to Venice in the 17th century. The city had survived previous outbreaks in 1348 and 1575 but the plague of 1630 was unprecedented in its scale of destruction. Estimates range from 20,000 to 90,000 deaths over a period of 14 months, with as many as 500 people dying every day at the height of the plague. In total, nearly a third of Venice was wiped out. And this time, unlike in previous outbreaks, the rich were affected in their palaces, just as the poor were in their tenements. Many noble Venetian families were completely annihilated in 1630.

Precautions were taken, such as assigning delegates to inspect the cleanliness of the homes of victims and closing public places such as churches and markets, but to little avail. Prisoners were pressed into service to carry and bury the increasing number of dead bodies but they could not keep up with the vast numbers in the end so barges were floated in the canals into which the bodies were thrown from the buildings above. People who had symptoms of the plague—foul smelling boils and pustules—but had not yet died were quarantined on the island of Lazzaretto Vecchio. Those who had been in contact with the infected were quarantined on the island of Lazzaretto Nuovo. In order to ensure compliance with the strict quarantines, a gallows was hastily constructed on a ship floating in the Grand Canal for nonconformers. Only doctors were allowed to circulate freely within the city.

The Plague Doctor

One of the most popular Carnival costumes in Venice is the eerie-looking 'plague doctor'. Consisting of a full-length, full-sleeved black coat, black hat, thin stick and trademark sinister-looking long, white bird beak with spectacles, it cuts a distinctive figure indeed. Few realise, however, that this 'costume' was once the gear of practicing physicians. Doctors during plague outbreaks wore such attire, usually soaked in oil or wax, for protection. The stick was for inspecting patients and moving back bedding without touching the afflicted. The sinister spectacled bird mask was for warding off evil spirits.

With all earthly means of disease control exhausted, the city leaders turned to the heavens for relief. Breaking their own edict to remain indoors, the disease-depleted Senate gathered for the unprecedented move of conducting a collective prayer to the Virgin Mary, asking for her intervention in the epidemic. The Senate vowed to construct a new, grand church in her honour should she take pity on Venice. Within a few weeks, newly reported cases of the plague had decreased to single digits. It was a miracle, at least to the surviving Venetians, and the next year the Senate made good on its promise.

A prime location was chosen for the new church—at the entrance to the Grand Canal opposite St. Mark's and adjacent to the Customs House at the end of the Dorsoduro. The Senate originally wanted Rome's famous Gian Lorenzo Bernini to construct the church but he declined. Therefore, the Senate opened up the project to a number of architects in the form of a design contest. Of the eleven finalists, they chose a relatively unknown Venetian architect, Baldassare Longhena, the son of a local stonemason. The 32-year-old architect described his design as "strange, worthy and beautiful…in the shape of a round machine".

The Feast of Health

The Feast of Health, or the *Festa della Salute*, was started in conjunction with the consecration of Longhena's church in 1687. The festival, which commemorates the intervention of the Virgin Mary in stopping the plague, continues to be celebrated today. On 21 November, a pontoon bridge is stretched out over the Grand Canal, connecting the church to the *sestiere* of San Marco.

Longhena, however, soon encountered serious problems with his design. The ground of the site was soft and waterlogged and could not support the weight of a structure so massive as the one he had planned. His solution? About 100,000 long wooden pilings that were driven deep into the bedrock of the lagoon. His next problem was how to support the weight of the massive church dome, which was modelled after St. Peter's in Rome. His solution was ingenious and can still be seen today in the sixteen massive curlicue braces that ring the supporting barrel beneath the dome. These functional braces look quite delicate and even whimsical but they give the Church of Santa Maria della Salute its distinctive look. Santa Maria della Salute, or simply Salute as the locals call it, took 50 years to complete, tragically five years longer than Longhena lived. Although the architect did not see it completed, the church dedicated to the Virgin Mary has endured as a testament to his vision and skill.

Another Death in Venice

Thomas Mann, noted author and one-time resident of Venice, described an epidemic of a different sort—cholera—in his famous novel *Death in Venice* (1912).

Designed by Baldassare Longhena, the Church of Santa Maria della Salute combines elements of Venetian Byzantine architecture with domes inspired by St. Peter's in Rome.

Gondolas

Squero San Trovaso, Rio di San Trovaso

Nothing in the world evokes the essence of Venice like the gondola. With a form that truly follows function, it is a craft unique in the world.

Venice is often described as being a city unique in the world. Equally unique then is the primary vehicle of Venice—the gondola. Dressed out in funerary black, gilded with its trademark saw-toothed blades at the prow and stern and propelled gracefully by a single oarsman, the gondola is the epitome of grace on water.

Gondolas have been plying the waters of Venice in one shape or another for close to a thousand years. The first mention of them comes from a decree from Doge Vitale Falier in 1094. But the vessel mentioned then probably bore little resemblance to the ones you see today.

From the 11th to 13th centuries, gondolas were described as being much larger craft that were often propelled by up to twelve oarsmen. By the Renaissance, the gondolas portrayed in paintings came much closer to the modern version—a long slender boat with upturned prow and stern that was propelled by a single oarsman. Over the next two centuries, gondolas were lengthened and slimmed down even further and the irons that decorated the prows and sterns began to be shaped in the way we are accustomed to seeing today. In the 17th century, gondolas were equipped with an enclosed passenger cover called a felze. The felze was large enough to accommodate several passengers and was often elaborately decorated and upholstered with silks and satins. The felze lent an air of mystery to the gondola as it offered privacy for illicit liaisons, clandestine transportation and even kidnappings. By the end of the 19th century, the felze had all but disappeared

The modern-day gondola is highly adapted for propulsion and guidance by a single upright oarsman. It is just under 11 metres (36 feet) long and just under 1.5 metres (58 inches) wide. It is also asymmetrical in that the port side is 24 centimetres (9.5 inches) longer than the right, giving the boat a slight crescent shape. This asymmetry also causes the gondola to sit unbalanced in the water until the gondolier steps into his position near the stern. Only then does the boat right itself. One might think that an asymmetrical boat would be difficult to steer and would tend to go in circles, but the shape actually compensates for the driving effect of an oar always working from the starboard side of the craft so that the gondola will track true. The one-of-a-kind shape of today's gondola can be attributed to Domenico Tramontin, a *squerariolo*, or gondola builder, from the late 19th century, who experimented with designs to improve the speed and manoeuvrability of the Venetian boats.

Paint It Black

In the 1500s, the gondola evolved, for a time, from a mere method of transportation to a tool of ostentation as wealthy Venetians tried to outdo one another in the decoration of their gondolas. These displays of wild colours, gilding and upholstery eventually prompted an edict from the Senate in 1562, decreeing that all gondolas be painted black.

The modern gondola is constructed to a strict standard using 280 separate pieces of wood. Using a multitude of woods such as fir, elm, oak, walnut, beech, cherry, larch, lime and mahogany, the master

Elegant gondolas on the Grand Canal.

gondola builder uses ancient, time-tested techniques, including alternating soaking and applied fire, to bend and shape the planks to give the boat its distinctive shape. From a single piece of either walnut or cherry wood, he then crafts the distinctive, elbow-shaped oarlock called the *forcola*. The forcola's twisted shape allows the gondolier to use his oar in eight different positions to manoeuvre the craft. The trademark prow decorations are highly symbolic of Venice. They are always the same regardless of which craftsman constructs the gondola. The sweeping blade at the top is designed to resemble the curved *corno*, or Doge's crown. The six forward-facing teeth below represent the six *sestieri*, or neighbourhoods, of the city, while the rear-facing tooth symbolises the island of Giudecca. The gondola is ready once seven coats of black lacquer have been applied, giving the boat its glossy finish.

Squero San Trovaso is not open to the public but you can get a good look at the works from the other side of the canal.

All work to build or repair a gondola is performed in a specialised workshop called a *squero*. In these squeri, the traditional knowledge of gondola construction is passed from father to son and from master to apprentice. Many fear, however, that the gondola and the squeri are dying out. In the 1800s, the number of gondolas in Venice numbered well into the thousands, today only 400 gondoliers are registered to operate within the city. Furthermore, there were dozens of squeri just 200 years ago but now there are only three. The most picturesque squero is San Trovaso, where the canals of Rio di San Trovaso and Rio Ognissanti meet.

Fathers and Sons

Gondoliers once numbered nearly ten thousand but now comprise a rarefied caste of a scant four hundred. Being a gondolier is a family-centred business with a son usually following his father's oar strokes (there has never been a recorded female gondolier). Almost all modern gondoliers speak some English and all are required to pass an exam on the basic history of the major sights in the city. Like cabbies in large cities, their knowledge of obscure canals and addresses is the stuff of legend. There is a race of gondoliers in the Grand Canal every year during Venice's summer regatta.

Inquisitive Art Critics

Feast in the House of Levi, Gallerie dell'Accademia

A famous painter executes a dramatic masterpiece but his inclusion of some odd characters draws the ire of the dreaded Inquisition.

In centuries past, the visual arts of painting, fresco and sculpture held far more sway than they do today. In their day, they were often much more than just aesthetic works of art. This was especially true for the Catholic Church, the main commissioner of artworks in Renaissance and baroque Italy. For instance, a painting commissioned by the Church was designed to inspire, entertain and, most important of all, instruct. The Renaissance and baroque artists of Italy were invited to execute works that were designed to illustrate biblical stories or analogies for the masses in churches throughout the country. In a manner of speaking, these artworks acted as the mass media of their day. Consequently, to the leaders of the Church, the artworks had to be historically accurate and true to the scriptures, otherwise the meaning would be lost or, perhaps worse, misinterpreted. As a rule, communications and, more importantly, expectations were consistent between artists and church officials, but not always.

The son of a stonecutter, Paolo Caliari was born in Verona in 1528. He later became known as Veronese after his birthplace. At an early age, Veronese abandoned his apprenticeship in his father's guild and took up painting. He proved a natural talent and went on to gain success painting altarpieces for churches in northern Italy.

Veronese moved to Venice at the age of 25. Venice offered him a world of possibilities and new commissions, as well as one major challenge. By moving to Venice, Veronese, an outsider, had to gain access into a field that already hosted giants such as Titian and Tintoretto. Fortunately for Veronese, his talent equalled the task. Within a few years, he had gained valuable and prestigious commissions in the Church of San Sebastiano and in the Doge's Palace. His future seemed bright and bigger commissions came his way, including a commission by the Church of Santi Giovanni e Paolo in 1573 to replace a work by Titian that had been destroyed in a fire in the church two years earlier. The theme of the commissioned painting was the Last Supper.

The Church of Santi Giovanni e Paolo is regarded by most as second only to St. Mark's Basilica and its reconstruction after the fire was considered a project of major importance to the island. Veronese discussed the commission with the friars of the church and then set to work on an enormous 6- x 14-metre canvas. When the artist presented the painting to the friars later that year, a controversy soon ensued.

The enormous painting is a masterwork to be sure. A divine Christ is centred amid a rabble of activity under a multi-arched portico of strong neoclassical Palladian design. The viewer's eye is first drawn to the seated Christ but soon wanders to take in the dizzying array of other characters and activities that fill the large scene. Moving out from the centre, you find the twelve apostles. However, the crowd seems to become more degenerate the further you move out: a man picking his teeth, a servant with a bleeding nose, turbaned Turks, German soldiers with halberds drinking, a midget jester with a parrot, Veronese himself as a self portrait and two mongrel dogs. It was hardly viewed as a reverent work.

The lead friar of the church was not pleased with the result and asked the artist to, at the very least, replace the dog in the foreground with a representation of Mary Magdalene. Veronese refused, stating that the work would remain as he had painted it.

On 18 July 1573, Veronese was summoned to the Church of San Teodoro to face the Holy Tribunal of the Inquisition.

It is hard to appreciate now how a few odd characters in a painting could cause such a stir as to merit a summons before the Inquisition but, in 16th-century Italy, Veronese's actions were tantamount to heresy.

Some 46 years earlier, in 1527, enraged Protestants from Germany, encouraged by Martin Luther and the excesses of the Catholic Church, had invaded Italy and sacked Rome. The Catholic Counter Reformation followed in which the Church involved itself fully in the works of artists (for purposes of piety, decency and accuracy, of course), even going so far as to have the nude characters in Michelangelo's *Last Judgment* repainted so that they were clothed. Veronese had painted the wrong work at the wrong time. As he appeared before the Inquisitors, his friends feared not only for the future of the great artist's career but also for his very life.

In a rare benefit of bureaucracy, the minutes of the short trial are chronicled in a Venetian State archived document. After a few preliminary questions, the Inquisitors got to the root of the issue by asking Veronese about the significance of the man with the nosebleed and the German soldiers. Veronese, seeing where this line of questioning was going, quickly interjected that painters use the same licence as poets and madmen and that he had added them from his own imagination. The Inquisitors next asked about the jester with a parrot on his wrist. Veronese replied that he was merely an ornament designed to take up the ample space on the canvas, as were the other characters. The Inquisitors then turned up the heat by asking Veronese if he thought it suitable to depict buffoons, drunken Germans, dwarfs and other such absurdities in a painting portraying the Last Supper. He was also asked if he thought it appropriate to paint pictures full of absurdities in order to ridicule the Church and teach false doctrine to the masses, as they were doing in Germany and other countries full of heresy. Veronese agreed that this was wrong and that this had not been his intention; he had merely needed to fill a very large canvas with characters. The members of the Tribunal finally decreed Veronese free to go but on the condition that he correct his *Last Supper* painting within three months, removing the offending oddities at his own expense.

Veronese devised a clever solution, not satisfying in the least the friars of the Church of Santi Giovanni e Paolo. Instead of correcting the offending figures, he simply changed the title of the painting to *Feast*

Veronese included himself quite prominently in the Feast in the House of Levi. *He is dressed in black and green and is standing at the left edge of the central portico with his arms held wide as if inviting even more outlandish characters into the scene.*

in the House of Levi. Thereby removing the initial cause for concern, the inaccurate portrayal of the Lord's Last Supper.

A French Prize

Veronese's *Last Supper*, later renamed *Feast in the House of Levi*, was one of the hundreds of priceless artworks plundered by French soldiers after the city surrendered to Napoleon in 1797. The painting was returned, as were many others (but not all), in 1815.

Palladio's Triptych

Giudecca: Churches of San Giorgio Maggiore, Santa Maria delle Zitelle and Il Redentore

A stonemason with an eye for the architecture of the ancients single-handedly revives classical design and forever leaves his mark on Venice.

The European Renaissance is one of the most fascinating periods in history as, in many ways, Western civilisation was rediscovered after centuries of darkness and many ancient arts were reincarnated to their former glory. One facet of this rediscovery was architecture. Outside of Venice, medieval architecture in the rest of Italy was largely uninspired but the Renaissance and a new appreciation for all things Greek and Roman breathed new life (or perhaps more accurately, old life) back into the art. As older examples of ancient Greek and Roman buildings were once again strewn throughout Italy, one young man noticed them and saw not history but potential.

Andrea di Pietro della Gondola was born in the Venetian territory of Padua in 1508 but he later became better known to the world as Andrea Palladio. At age 13, Andrea became an apprentice to a workshop of stonecutters in Padua but fled to nearby Vicenza three years later to join another workshop of stonemasons. He worked humbly in this field until a timely introduction to the humanist poet and scholar Gian Giorgio Trissino of Vicenza changed his life forever.

Andrea met Trissino when the latter was designing an addition to his villa outside Vicenza. Trissino took an immediate interest in the young stonemason and began to tutor him in the rediscovered principles of ancient architecture, including the rediscovered classical architectural texts of Vitruvius. Trissino saw the talent in his new pupil and endeavoured to give him a name worthy of it. He named the budding architect Palladio after the Palladium, the statue of the Greek god Pallas Athena, which was spirited to Rome by Aeneas after the fall of Troy.

Andrea took to the name and to the classics. He travelled to Rome at least three times, during which his passion for the past was solidified upon seeing the magnificence of the city's ancient buildings. He began to use classical architectural elements in his early commissions, which were secured through Trissino. Over the next decade, Palladio became the premier architect in the Veneto outside of Venice, specialising in large country villas of neoclassical design. Interestingly, while he designed and executed many country villas for rich Venetians, Palladio did not get any work within the city until he was nearly in his sixties.

At the age of 58, in 1560, the renowned Palladio finally received his first commission within Venice. He was asked to design the refectory of the Benedictine monastery of San Giorgio at the far western end of the island of Giudecca, off Dorsoduro. This first work led to a huge commission five years later to design and build the Church of San Giorgio Maggiore.

Standing on an island across St. Mark's basin and directly opposite St. Mark's Square, the Church of San Giorgio Maggiore is yet another landmark of Venice. Palladio won the commission for the project in 1565 and the building was essentially completed 11 years later (although

The façade of the Church of San Giorgio Maggiore.

it would take another 35 years for the marble façade of Palladio's trademark columns and triangular pediments to be completed).

Mixed Opinions

Palladio's designs have always spawned sharp opinions. Some regard him as a bold new thinker; others, at best, think him a mimicking recycler of ideas. In *The Stones of Venice*, 19th-century traveller and writer John Ruskin said of Palladio's Church of San Giorgio Maggiore: "It is impossible to conceive a design more gross, more barbarous, more childish in conception, more servile in plagiarism, more insipid in result, more contemptible under every point of rational regard." In contrast, Goethe credited Palladio with throwing away the vestiges of the medieval era.

Just to the east of San Giorgio Maggiore on the Giudecca is the relatively small (compared to San Giorgio Maggiore) church of Santa Maria delle Zitelle, or simply La Zitelle for short. This is another magnificent example of Palladio's neoclassical churches in Venice. It was designed

Palladio's Church of Santa Maria delle Zitelle stands in front of the Grand Canal.

by the architect after the site was purchased in 1561 but construction did not begin until after Palladio's death in 1580. It was completed in 1586.

The Four Books

Ten years before his death, Palladio published a comprehensive masterwork of his thoughts on architecture, *I Quattro Libri* (*The Four Books*). This book outlined his design and architectural principles as well as offered practical advice for builders (no doubt drawing on his early years as a stonemason). Palladio's book was reprinted in English and became the basis for the revival movement in neoclassical architecture in the 18th century, which can be seen from the estates of England to the monuments in Washington D. C.

Further to the east, along the Fondamenta San Giacomo, lies another Palladian masterpiece—the Church of Il Redentore, or the Redeemer. This church, like the Church of Santa Maria della Salute, was commissioned and constructed in an attempt to relieve the city from a plague epidemic. From 1575 to 1577, Venice was in the grip of a plague outbreak that claimed over 50,000 lives. As an offering for divine intervention, the Senate decreed a church to be built in the hope of deliverance. Many architects submitted designs but Palladio's was chosen. The foundation stone was laid in May 1577 and two months later, on 20 July, the end of the plague outbreak was officially celebrated.

Although located on the island of Giudecca, the Church of Il Redentore is visible from the piazzetta of St. Mark's.

Although Palladio died in 1580, Il Redentore was finished in the relatively quick time of 15 years, with Antonio da Ponte, the architect of the Rialto Bridge, completing the project.

The Feast of the Redeemer

With the celebration of the end of the plague on 20 July 1577, a new holiday was born in Venice and it survives to this day (although it is now marked annually on the third Sunday in July). The Feast of the Redeemer, or *Festa del Redentore*, is celebrated with a procession from the Zattere to the Church of Il Redentore on a pontoon bridge, followed by evening fireworks.

INSIDER'S TIPS

Gallerie dell'Accademia   Once Venice's art school and now converted into a first-class gallery, the Accademia is one of the city's must-see sights. Works by Carpaccio, Titian, Tintoretto and Veronese, among others, are here. Euro 6.50. Open 8.15am–2pm Monday, 8.15am–7.15pm Tuesday to Sunday (Last entrance 30 minutes before closing). Ponte di Accademia. Tel: 041 5222247. Website: www. galleriaaccademia.org/

The Peggy Guggenheim Collection   Peggy Guggenheim moved to Venice in 1949 and set up in Palazzo Venier dei Leoni where she was able to amass an amazing collection of modern art until her death in 1979. She is buried in the garden. Euro 10. Open 10am–6pm. Closed Tuesday. Palazzo Venier dei Leoni. Website: www.guggenheim-venice. it/english/

Church of Santa Maria della Salute   This church was built in honour of the Virgin Mary following the end of the 1630–1631 plague. Of note inside are the works by Titian in the sacristy and Tintoretto's *Wedding at Cana*. Free. Open daily 9am–noon, 3.30pm–6pm. Campo della Salute. Website: www.marcianum.it/salute/

Church of Santa Maria del Rosario   Commonly known as the Gesuati, this Palladian-style church is home to the city's Dominicans. Facing the Giudecca, the church contains a couple of interesting Tiepolos. Of interest two doors down at the Church of Santa Maria della Visitazione is one of the few remaining Lion's Mouth denunciation letterboxes, which were used during the Venetian republic. Euro 2.50 or Chorus Pass. Open 10am–5pm Monday to Saturday, 1pm–5pm Sunday. Fondamenta della Zattere ai Gesuati.

Church of San Trovaso   This quiet neighbourhood church contains a respectable collection inside, including three paintings by Jacopo and Domenico Tintoretto and two altarpieces by Palma the Younger. Free. Open 3pm–6pm Monday to Saturday. Campo San Trovaso.

Squero San Trovaso This quaint site with chalet-type buildings and a sloping entrance into the Canal San Trovaso is one of only three operating gondola construction and repair workshops in the city. It is not open to the public but you can get a good look from this side of the canal. Fondamenta Nani.

Church of San Sebastiano Tucked into a little visited corner of the city, this neighbourhood church is truly one of the city's most overlooked treasures. San Sebastiano is decorated with a stunning array of works by Veronese. Titian also found his way in for one work. Veronese is buried in this church at the foot of the organ. Euro 2 or Chorus Pass. Open 10am–5pm Monday to Saturday, 1pm–5pm Sunday. Campo di San Sebastiano.

Church of San Giorgio Maggiore This church is one of Palladio's masterpieces and a landmark in the city skyline. Inside you will find a couple of interesting Tintorettos and a Carpaccio (not always on display). Free. Open daily 9am–noon, 2pm–6pm in the summer. It is only open in the afternoon during the winter. Island of San Giorgio Maggiore.

Church of Il Redentore Another of Palladio's churches in Venice, Il Redentore (The Redeemer) was built as a response to a plague outbreak from 1575 to 1577. Inside you will find works by Bassano, Tintoretto and Veronese. Euro 2.50 or Chorus Pass. Open 10am–5pm Monday to Saturday, 1pm–5pm Sunday. Campo del SS Redentore.

Ca della Corte Looking for something a little different or off the beaten track? Then why not try a nice bed and breakfast in Venice. The Ca della Corte offers doubles with bathroom for Euro 85–165 and luxury suites complete with pianos for Euro 150–230 (discounts for extended stays). The manager, Annarosa, can even organise a wedding if you want to get married in Venice. This B&B is one of the few establishments in the city to offer a handicapped-accessible apartment for four to six people. English-language babysitters are available. Corte Surian. Tel: 041 715877. Website: www.cadellacorte.com

Hotel Pausania Try staying in a converted palazzo. The Pausania is well run and tastefully decorated with period artworks. Fondamenta Gerardini 2824. Tel: 041 5333083. Website: www.hotelpausania.it

Ostello Venezia This is Venice's youth hostel, open only to holders of IYHF or AIG cards. A bed with breakfast costs Euro 18.50 but you will have to use the rather expensive public transport to get to the main island from here (*see* Travel Facts for further details). Fondamenta delle Zitelle (Giudecca) 86. Tel: 041 5238211. Website: www.ostellionline. org/ostello.php?idostello=236

Aquarama Open only for dinner, the Aquarama rivals the high-brow restaurant at Hotel Cipriani for its menu and quality of food, at about half the price and with twice as better service. Chef Antonio is a magician with seafood. One of the best restaurants in the city. Euro 15–25 per plate. Fondamenta Zattere Ponte Lungo. Tel: 041 5206601.

Trattoria Osteria Venessiana You know you are eating at a locals-only restaurant if the menu is only in Italian. Don't worry, the staff speak some English and whatever you order will be delicious. Euro 10–15 per plate for great local seafood. Fondamenta Tre Ponti. Tel: 041 710749.

65 Pizza A great takeaway pizza shop that sells pizza by the slice. Very popular with the locals. 65 Calle Vinanti.

Café Blue A good local pub with friendly staff. Open late for Venice. Calle dei Preti Crosera/Calle San Pantalon.

Vinus Venezia The best *enoteca* (wine bar) in this neighbourhood. Good appetizers, too. Calle Scalater.

Tonolo The best *pasticceria* in this neighbourhood and perhaps the best in Venice. Always full of Venetians. Calle San Pantalon.

Gobbetti This is another good *pasticceria.* Just north of Ponte dei Pugni.

Calle San Pantalon This street offers good shopping at a fraction of San Marco prices.

Loris Marazzi (Scultore di Madera) Local sculptor Loris turns everyday items into wood with dramatic results. Campo Santa Margherita.

Le Forcole You read in this section about where gondolas are made. This is where the *forcolas*, or oarlocks, are made by hand by Saverio Pastor. He makes them for gondolas as well as for gifts. Fondamenta di Cabala. Tel: 041 5225699. Website: www.forcole.com

Mondo Novo This is a first-class mask shop that has been run by noted artist Gerrino Lovato for 20 years. You can see the artist working on site. North of Ponte dei Pugni (just south of Campo Santa Margerita). Tel: 041 5287344.

Gondolas If you hire a gondola in Venice, be prepared to reach deep into your wallet as a 50-minute gondola ride will set you back Euro 71, rising to Euro 90 for 50 minutes after dark. It can make for an unforgettable experience if you can afford it but make the most of your fare and skip the Grand Canal, which you can see from the deck of a Vaporetto, or ferry bus, for Euro 3.50. Instead, opt to hire a gondolier on the Grand Canal and have him explore the back canals of your favourite neighbourhood, mine is San Polo.

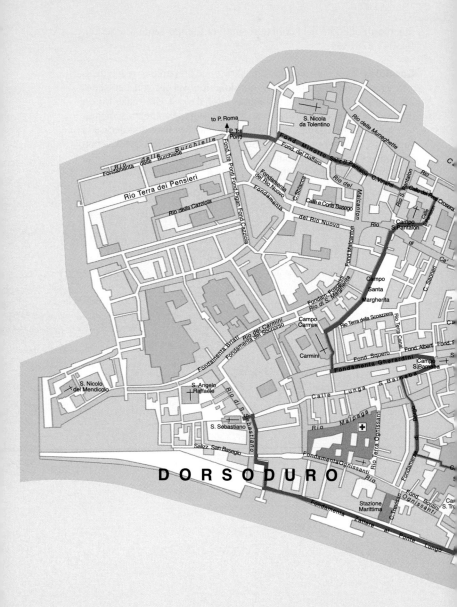

Short Walk

Starting Point—Piazzale Roma. Walk down Fondamenta Cossetti until you reach the Ponte Tre Ponti. Once you cross the bridge, you will find yourself on the Fondamenta Magazen. Go straight until you reach another bridge. Cross over the bridge. Take the first left and then the first right onto Fondamenta Minotto. This fondamenta turns into the Saliz. San Pantalon and then into the Calle Vinanti. Once you cross the Rio San Pantalon, the street turns into the Calle dei Preti Crosera. Turn left into the Calle San Pantalon. Walk through the Campo San Pantalon, cross the Rio di Ca' Foscari and follow the Calle dei Chiesa to the Campo Santa Margherita.

Follow the Campo Santa Margarita to the end where you will come across the Church of I Carmini. Follow the church to the left and cross the Rio di San Barnaba. Turn left and follow the Fondamenta Gherardini until you reach the Campo San Barnaba. Cross the campo and turn left. Then take Calle d. Turchette, which turns into Fondamenta di Borgo. Turn into C. Occhiatera, which turns into C. d. Chiesa. Cross the bridge and walk along Fondamenta Nani until you reach the Fondamenta Zattere Ponte Lungo. Turn right and walk along the fondamenta until you reach Calle dei Vento. Turn right and you will find yourself in the Campo San Basegio. Walk to the end of the campo and follow the Fondamenta San Basilio. Cross the Rio di San Sebastiano to get to the Campo San Sebastian. There you will find the Church of San Sebastiano.

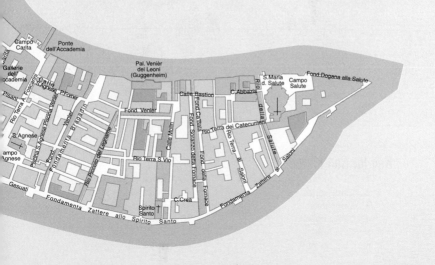

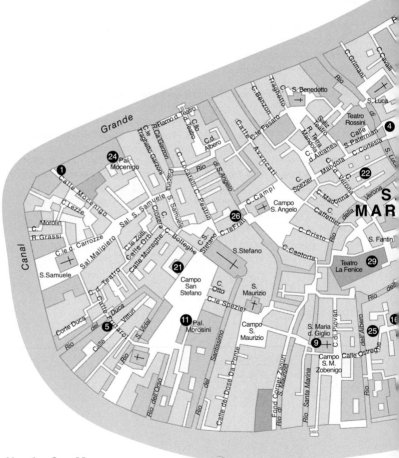

Key for San Marco

1. Ca' Mocenigo Casa Vecchia
2. Caffé Florian
3. Campanile
4. Campo Manin
5. Casa Arte
6. Chet qui rit

7. Church of San Moise
8. Church of San Salvador
9. Church of Santa Maria del Giglio
10. Doge's Palace
11. Fiorella Gallery
12. Harry's Bar

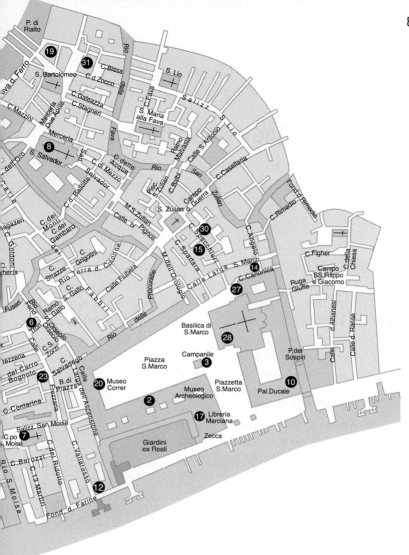

13. Hotel Centauro
14. Hotel Concordia
15. Hotel Panada
16. Hotel Saturnia
17. Library of St. Mark's
18. Linda Gonzales
19. Mille Vini
20. Museo Correr
21. NetHouse
22. Osteria Ai Assassini

23. Osteria Enoteca
24. Palazzo Mocenigo
25. Petra
26. Rigattieri
27. Sottoportego del Cappello
28. St. Mark's Basilica
29. Teatro La Fenice
30. Trattoria Do Forni
31. Vivaldi Store

Body Snatchers

Sarcophagus of St. Mark, St. Mark's Basilica

A new city is rising but its inhabitants are not happy with their patron saint. Their solution? Steal a better one.

Venice is the upstart of Italian cities. Becoming a proper city only in the 8th century, it lagged behind Milan, Florence and certainly Rome in historical and religious precedence. This nagged at the nascent city as it quickly grew. Venice seemed destined to always be the latecomer to the party if something was not done about it. So by incorporating revisionist history, divine predestination, some myth, some truth and a little grave robbing, the Venetians got their man, or rather their saint.

Second-place Saint: Theodore

St. Mark was not the first saint of Venice. That 'honour' (as it was dishonourable to demote him) went to St. Theodore, the patron saint of soldiers. His statue can still be seen standing atop his dragon (which looks more like a crocodile) atop one of the two columns in St. Mark's Square.

Venetian legend has it that St. Mark the Evangelist stopped at the cluster of islands that now comprise Venice in the 1st century. While in the lagoon, Mark had a dream in which an angel stated the enigmatic "Peace be with you Mark, my evangelist. Here, your body will rest." Although Mark went on to preach in the region of Veneto before travelling to Rome, where he wrote his gospel, this dream became a cornerstone for identifying St. Mark with Venice. Mark eventually travelled to North Africa and settled in the port city of Alexandria in

Egypt, where he set up a church before being martyred in A.D. 68. Mark was entombed in the city where he laid in peace until 828.

By 828, Alexandria was no longer a Christian city but a Muslim one and Christian relics no longer enjoyed divine status, a fact that was to provide the perfect opportunity for a pair of enterprising Venetians. History, albeit loosely, records Tribuno da Malamocco and Rustico da Torcello sailing to Alexandria (perhaps on the orders of the Doge) to steal the body of St. Mark in 828. Once the Venetians arrived at their destination, they presented the Christian guardians of Mark's tomb with the idea of spiriting the saint's remains out of Alexandria and out of Muslim hands. The local priests, fearing for the sanctity of their church and their relics, agreed to the idea. The tomb was opened and the burial shroud was slit open at the back to remove Mark's body. The body of St. Claudian, taken from a nearby tomb, was reportedly put in the shroud as a replacement. Mark's body was then placed in a large basket and carried down to the dock where da Malamocco and da Torcello's ship awaited. However, Egyptian heat and corpses make for an aromatic combination and suspicions had been aroused by the time they had reached their ship. The quick-thinking Venetians cleverly covered Mark's body with strong spices and sides of pork. When the customs officers came to investigate, the Venetians threw back the cover of the basket to reveal the sides of pork to the Muslim officials. The Muslims recoiled at the unclean sight and allowed the Venetians to depart. All three men arrived in Venice, where da Malamocco and da Torcello presented Mark to the Doge. Doge Participazio received the saint's remains and ordered the immediate construction of a basilica—St. Mark's Basilica—to house and honour the Evangelist.

Following the theft of the saint's remains, the Venetians were quick to justify their actions. They emphasised the need to protect the saintly remains from Muslim marauders. They also went so far as to draw a liberal interpretation of Mark's dream in the lagoon, claiming that it was divine predestination that Mark be brought to Venice where he would find his promised rest.

St. Mark's Basilica symbolises the Venetian lagoon and encapsulates the city's history.

Regardless of the reason or the later justification, the theft of St. Mark put Venice squarely on the map. If a patron saint was good, a fully fledged Evangelist on par with Paul, Matthew and John and the apostle Peter was better.

Mutual Protection

The relationship between St. Mark and the Doge of Venice was an interesting one. Whenever a new Doge was elected, the first thing he did was sign a contract called a *promissione*, in which, on behalf of the citizens of Venice, the Doge swore to protect the sanctity of Mark's new tomb in exchange for Mark's protection over the city.

St. Mark immediately put Venice on the same religious footing as Rome. No longer was Venice beholden to the pope and his St. Peter for Christian favour. The city now had St. Mark and his agent, the Doge. Many have credited the theft of St. Mark and his continuing preservation by the Doge (a secular and not a religious leader) as the seminal element in the foundation of Venetian independence. Venice was an upstart no more.

The remains of St. Mark were initially buried in a chapel in the Doge's Palace but were moved to St. Mark's Basilica once the construction of the church was complete.

The Lions of Venice: St. Mark as the Winged Lion

Wherever you go in Venice, you will see lions. These lions are often winged. The lion, and specifically the winged lion, has been interpreted as a symbolic representation for Mark in the Bible. In the book of Ezekiel (1:10) and Revelations (4:7), there are references to four creatures: an ox, an eagle, a man and a lion. Each of the four Evangelists is associated with one of these creatures: Luke with the ox because he describes how Jesus was born in a manger; John with the eagle because of his soaring presentation of Christ as the Word; Matthew with the man because of his humanist gospel; and Mark with the lion because his gospel opens with a scene in the wilderness. Often, St. Mark's winged lion is portrayed with a paw holding an open book on which is written *Pax tibi Marce, evangelista meus* (Peace be with you Mark, my evangelist).

Bruno's Ghost

Ca' Mocenigo Casa Vecchia

A radical philosopher is mistaken for a sorcerer and is denounced to the Inquisition, with fatal (and some say, haunting) results.

Venice has always been a haven for freethinkers, nonconformists and libertines. Casanova, Galileo, Lord Byron and Ernest Hemingway are just a few who have called the city home for a time. But even free Venice has its limits and once these limits are crossed the consequences can often be disastrous, as was the case for a little-known, forward-thinking philosopher at the height of the Renaissance.

Born near Naples in 1548, Giordano Bruno was a child of the Renaissance. Possessing an inquisitive and ever-questioning mind, he could not have been born at a better time or, at least, it seemed. In this time of intellectual awakening and rediscovery, nearly everything was up for grabs as far as ideas were concerned.

Bruno joined the Order of St. Dominic at the age of 17, where he began his education in earnest. But Bruno was a poor Dominican. He was independent in spirit and removed all the pictures of saints from his quarters in the monastery. He formed his own opinions and voiced them to his colleagues and instructors. His inquisitive mind also drew him towards forbidden texts. One of the authors he secretly studied was pioneer astronomer Copernicus, the innovator of the heliocentric theory (the theory that the Earth orbits around the Sun and that the Sun is the centre of our solar system). It was a radical idea and only a little over 20 years old when Bruno first read it. At age 28, the outspoken Bruno wrote a satirical play in which he reflected the hypocrisy and depravity of the monastery. He was charged with heresy and would have been brought before the Inquisition had he not fled from the Dominican Order, excommunicated, to wander throughout Europe.

The next 15 years of his life took him to England, France and Germany where he studied, taught and wrote about 20 books on science, philosophy and memory technique. Bruno's intellect was keen and no doubt obvious to the universities that sought him, including Oxford. However, Bruno's questioning mind and stubborn will eventually put him at odds with these institutions. It was a character flaw that was to dog Bruno his entire life. He was always so certain that he was right and always so confident in his ability to explain his truth to others that he could not fathom that anyone might hold other opinions, let alone disagree with him over them. One by one, the universities of Europe, including Geneva, Paris, Oxford, Cambrai, Wittenberg and Zurich, invited and then asked him to leave.

By 1591, Bruno was living in Frankfurt working as a freelance teacher and lecturer, mainly trading on a combination of philosophy and demonstrations of his prodigious memory. These public feats of memory were the fruits of several years of dedication and authorship on the subject. These memory demonstrations were quite popular among 16th-century Europeans but many thought his feats to be the fruits of sorcery rather than scholarship. It was exactly this type of misunderstanding that brought Bruno to his end.

Word of his skills and knowledge became known to a pair of Italian book merchants who befriended Bruno and took copies of his works to Venice to sell. Back in Venice, the controversial books piqued the interest of a young Venetian nobleman, Giovanni Mocenigo. Mocenigo immediately inquired of the booksellers where the author could be found and sent an invitation to Bruno in Germany. Mocenigo wanted to be instructed in the art of memory and other topics and invited Bruno to stay as a guest in his Venetian palazzo, the Ca' Mocenigo Casa Vecchia, on the Grand Canal. Returning to Italy would be a risk for Bruno but he assumed that he would be safe given that Venice was a republic independent from Rome. His assumption was wrong.

Not Right for the Job

When Giordano Bruno first arrived in Venice on Giovanni Mocenigo's invitation, he applied for the vacant chair in mathematics at the nearby University of Padua. Although he taught there briefly, the chair was given to another candidate, a younger man named Galileo.

Shortly after arriving at the Ca' Mocenigo Casa Vecchia, Giovanni Mocenigo turned the tables on Bruno and demanded to be taught all the philosopher knew about the dark arts of magic. Bruno professed his ignorance of such nonsense and began to embark on discourses of science and mnemonics. When Bruno declared his intentions to return to Frankfurt to publish some new works, Mocenigo became jealous that his

Ca' Mocenigo Casa Vecchia—the palazzo where Bruno entered a guest but left a prisoner.

tutor would impart his precious knowledge to others and not him. Mocenigo demanded to be taught the secrets that Bruno knew about power and magic or else he threatened to denounce Bruno to the Inquisition. Bruno again pleaded his ignorance and prepared to leave for Germany the next day. That night, Mocenigo, along with six hired gondoliers, burst into Bruno's room, removed him and locked him in an upper room of the palazzo. Giovanni Mocenigo gave Bruno one last chance to share his knowledge. Bruno claimed that he had done nothing wrong and demanded to be released. He was released, but into the custody of the Venetian Inquisition.

Bruno's Infinite Worlds

In 16th-century Europe, most notably in the eyes of conservative popes, the Earth was the centre of the universe. Bruno knew better and had the courage to profess it but this declaration eventually cost him his life. According to Bruno, the Earth was not the centre of everything but instead revolved around the Sun, which was one of many stars. The problem for the Church was that it followed that the infinite number of stars in God's creation should all have planets such as the Earth in their respective orbits and that these planets, too, had been created by God and would be populated with divine creations made in his image, namely more humans like us. Bruno took it further in that it was likely that each of these planets hosted a Garden of Eden and that in these gardens, half the Adams and Eves had partaken of the forbidden fruit, but half had not. Half of infinity, however, was still an infinity; therefore an infinite number of worlds would fall from grace, as did ours. Further, if the coming of Christ and His death on Earth was mandated by our fall, then it would be mandated an infinite number of times on these other 'fallen' worlds as well. Now either there was one Jesus who ventured from world to world atoning for sins through His death or there existed a plurality of Christs who did the same on their respective worlds. Since a single Jesus atoning for sins on an infinite number of worlds would take an infinite amount of time, God must have, therefore, created an infinite number of Christs to redeem these infinite worlds.

The Venetian Inquisitors heard a long list of accusations from Mocenigo and others, but try as they might, torture included, they could not get Bruno to confess to sorcery. When the supreme inquisitor, Cardinal Santaseverina of Rome, heard of Bruno's capture in Venice, he asked that the renegade Dominican be turned over to papal authorities for further investigation. Venice at first declined but eventually acceded to the cardinal's demands. Bruno was sent to Rome, where he was tried as a heretic and burned at the stake in 1600.

However, that was not the last that Giovanni Mocenigo saw of Giordano Bruno as Bruno is said to have haunted the Mocenigo family home ever since.

Casanova's Escape

Casanova's cell, I Piombi (The Leads Prison), Doge's Palace

*The world's most famous libertine is brought before
the Inquisition, then thrown into Venice's notorious
'Leads' prison, only to execute a brilliant escape.*

Venice, like many Italian cities of the age, had a complex justice system and often overlapping civil and religious authorities. The courts convicted petty criminals and debtors, the Doge and his agents imprisoned opponents, the secretive Council of Ten incarcerated plotters and investigated threats to the state and the Inquisition often locked up whomever it pleased. All of the condemned, however, had the same end point, Venice's notorious pair of prisons, I Pozzi and I Piombi. I Pozzi, or "The Wells" in English, was so named because it comprised dank, dark and often flooded cells at the bottom of the Doge's Palace. I Piombi, or "The Leads" in English, was so named because its cells were located on the top floor of the palace, just beneath the heavy lead shingle roof. The conditions of both prisons were horrible. Oppressively hot in the summer and freezing cold in the winter, the small cells, most of which were less than 140 centimetres (4.6 feet) high so that a man could not stand upright, were plagued by mosquitoes, fleas and enormous rats. Many entered these two notorious prisons but few ever left alive and only four are ever recorded to have escaped. Two of these prisoners escaped together from The Leads on 31 October 1756, one a slow-witted monk, the other the world-famous lover and libertine, Casanova.

Giovanni Giacomo Casanova was a native Venetian, born in 1725 in a home near the Campo San Samuele. Casanova had once considered a career of the cloth until his first sensual adventures convinced him against such a folly. By his early twenties, Casanova had begun down the licentious road that would make him a household name. Within a few months of his 30th birthday, his actions and reputation would lead him into the hands of the Inquisition.

By 1755, Casanova was living a hedonistic life, driven by gambling, women and thinking of ways to pay for more of both. In July of that year, he happened to meet a precious stone merchant named Manuzzi who offered Casanova the opportunity to purchase diamonds on credit. The stone merchant visited Casanova at home and noted that he had several interesting books on the occult. Manuzzi told Casanova that he knew a man who would pay highly for such volumes and asked if he could borrow them to show the potential buyer. Casanova agreed and the engine of his doom was set in motion. Manuzzi was actually a spy in the employ of the office of the Inquisition, where he promptly took Casanova's books. The Inquisitors made no delay and sent a party of 40 officers to arrest Casanova on charges of sorcery (although it was more likely for making a cuckold of many Venetian nobles). The guards took him to a cell in The Leads.

The Bridge of Sighs

The Bridge of Sighs was built to connect the Doge's Palace to the Leads prison in 1614. The bridge's name was inspired by the sighs of prisoners as they saw Venice for the last time before being led away into the prison.

Casanova described his cell as "8 feet square with a $5^1/_2$-foot tall ceiling" devoid of any furnishings save a bucket, "the use of which may be guessed." With no trial, no formal sentence and no thoughts save his own for company, Casanova quickly fell into a deep depression of which he would write later: "Alone in a gloomy cell where he only sees the fellow who brings his food once a day, where he cannot walk upright, he is the most wretched of men. He would like to be in hell, if he believes in it, for the sake of the company." He soon realised that he would have to escape or he would go mad. Yet escaping from a prison so fortified as The Leads would take more than Casanova's keen intellect; he would need luck, and that is exactly what he got.

This bolted door led to Casanova's cell in The Leads, his 'home' for 18 months.

After six months in The Leads, Casanova was on one of his rare visits to the hallway outside his cell when he noticed an iron bar lying in the corner. He swiftly grabbed it and hid it under his nightshirt. Back in his cell, he took the bar and began sharpening it against a piece of marble. In a short time, he had a tool that he could use to begin his escape. He then hollowed out one leg of his chair, in which he hid the tool. His plan was to make a hole in the wooden floor of the cell and use his bedding as a rope to lower himself into what he believed to be the Sala della Bussola, from where he could rush out as soon as the guards opened the doors in the morning. Within a few weeks, he had penetrated all but the last few millimetres of the floor. All he needed to do was wait for a feast day when he knew there would be fewer guards in the palace. The day before Casanova was to attempt his escape, his guard informed him that he was going to be moved to a more comfortable cell with a higher ceiling on the floor below.

Comforts of Home

Despite the horrific condition of the cells within The Leads, well-to-do inmates could purchase creature comforts such as books, outside meals, furniture and clothing.

Casanova was beside himself at the missed opportunity and could only begin to imagine the consequences once the guard discovered the hole. When the angry guard demanded to be given the tool used to make the hole, a quick-witted Casanova replied, "If it be true that I have made a hole at all, I shall say that you gave me the tools, and that I have returned them to you." The threat worked and Casanova's furniture was moved intact to his new cell, with it the sharpened iron bar. As his cell was now searched regularly, a similar escape plan seemed impossible. He needed a new plan.

Casanova knew he now needed an accomplice in another cell to help him escape and set about finding one. He argued to the guards that he and other inmates could save expenses on books by being allowed to exchange them among themselves. The guards agreed and Casanova began to enclose messages in the bindings of his books in search for a kindred spirit. He soon found one in a 38-year-old monk named Marin Balbi.

Balbi was in The Leads for fathering three children and then trying to baptise them. By luck, the monk was in the cell above Casanova's. Casanova told Balbi of his tool but that he would need another's help to attempt escape. Balbi would have to use the tool to break into Casanova's cell and then they could both escape via the roof with a foolproof plan that Casanova had verified would work. In fact, Casanova had no plan beyond Balbi breaking into his cell. Nevertheless, Balbi accepted the makeshift plan. The question now was how to get the tool to Balbi.

Casanova knew he would have to smuggle the tool to the monk in a book but the bar was nearly 60 centimetres (2 feet) long, much longer than any book that either of them possessed. Therefore, Casanova requested the guards to purchase him a newly printed edition of the Bible in the hope that the book would be large enough to conceal the tool. When the Bible arrived, Casanova discovered that the bolt stuck out slightly at both ends of the book. Undeterred, Casanova tuned the plan to perfection. He paid one of the guards to help him prepare a special meal of macaroni and cheese for his friend, Monk Balbi, for whom the Bible was intended. The guard agreed and brought a saucepan of boiling macaroni, the necessary seasonings and an enormous dish to Casanova's cell. Casanova prepared the dish, filling it to the brim with macaroni, melted butter and hot cheese. He then placed the dish carefully on top of the Bible, which barely concealed the tool, and handed the precarious combination to the guard, hoping he would be too focused on not spilling the butter onto the new Bible to not notice the iron bar. Casanova described the event in his memoirs: "As I gave him this weighty load I kept my eyes fixed on his, and I saw to my joy that he did not take his gaze off the butter, which he was afraid of spilling." Balbi received the bar and set to work immediately. Casanova did not delay this time and once Balbi had broken into his cell, they both set about escaping.

Now reunited with his trusted tool, Casanova used it to break through the riveted lead shingles in Balbi's cell. With a change of clothes in hand, Casanova and Balbi scrambled onto the roof. After searching several hours under the cover of night for a way down and Casanova confessing that he did not actually have a plan beyond the stage they were at, the two broke into an unsecured attic room. There, Casanova changed into his second set of cleaner clothes and the two made their way in the darkness down to the lower floor, where a guard spotted them and, mistaking them for officials locked inside from the evening before, opened the palace doors for them.

Casanova, with typical debonair aplomb, stopped for a cup of coffee in St. Mark's Square (the first in nearly 18 months), then the two hailed a gondola for the mainland and escaped as the sun was rising. Casanova recalled the moment clearly in his memoirs: "I then turned and looked at the entire length of the beautiful canal, and, seeing not a single boat, admired the most beautiful day one could hope for…"

Invention of the Lottery and Riches

Casanova managed to escape from The Leads and made his way to Paris, where he invented the concept of the lottery, an idea that made him rich.

Harry's Bar

Harry's Bar, Calle Vallaresso

A simple act of charity marks the beginning of a Venetian landmark.

What makes a restaurant or bar a landmark in a particular city? Longevity, quality, fame, celebrity status? Probably a combination of all of these things, but the most compelling factor is reputation. When someone says, "Oh, you're going to Rome, you must go to Alfredo's" or "Stopping off in Singapore? You must have a drink at Raffles", you will visit those places and, if satisfied, you will tell others. This makes a landmark. The landmark in Venice is Harry's Bar. Going to Venice? You must go to Harry's Bar.

The unassuming doors leading into Harry's Bar.

The story of Harry's Bar goes back to the early bartending career of a small Venetian named Giuseppe Cipriani. In 1929, Cipriani had been the bartender at the prestigious Hotel Europa for two years, looking after the well-heeled foreign clientele. And in the summer of 1929, there were many well-heeled foreigners in Venice. One was a young American from Boston named Harry Pickering. Pickering had been sent by his family to Europe to cure his binge drinking. The plan had failed miserably as Pickering spent nearly all his time with Cipriani in the Europa Bar. After several months, Pickering stopped spending as much time in the bar and drank less when he did. Cipriani asked the

American if anything was wrong. A depressed Pickering replied that he was broke. The young barman offered to lend Pickering enough money to pay off his bills and get him back to the United States. The sum total was 10,000 lire (then roughly US$5000)—a king's ransom for a simple bartender—but Cipriani lent him the money.

A few months later, in October, the U.S. stock market crashed. Fortunes were lost as the United States slid into the Great Depression. Undeterred, Cipriani knew in his heart that he had made the right decision and that the young American would be back. How right he was. The weeks dragged into months and the months into nearly two years but, in 1931, Pickering walked through the doors of the Hotel Europa Bar and changed Cipriani's life forever. He ordered a drink and placed 10,000 lire on the bar in front of Cipriani. In a further expression of his gratitude, Pickering laid another 40,000 lire on the bar, saying that the sum of money was for a bar that they would open together. They agreed to call it Harry's Bar. The rest is history but it's good history so I will continue.

Cipriani and Pickering found a location for Harry's Bar not far from St. Mark's Square. It was originally only a bar but quickly expanded into a full-service restaurant as well. One of the first customers to frequent Harry's on a regular basis, besides Harry himself, was a stuttering Englishman named Hawks. On his last night in Venice, Hawks stopped at Harry's for a drink and asked for directions to the garage at the Piazzale Roma. Cipriani, in another fortuitous moment of charity, said that if Hawks could wait until he had closed the bar he would escort him to the garage personally. Cipriani walked the Englishman across the city to the garage, explaining details of the city as they went.

Some weeks later, a patron came into Harry's with a copy of the London *Daily Mail* and pointed to an article:

"If you happen to be in Venice and want to know something about the city, forget the travel agencies and the tourist offices. Go to Harry's Bar. There you will find Giuseppe Cipriani, who can satisfy your every need…"

The byline was Colin Hawks. This was the first of many recommendations that served to jump start Harry's Bar. A few years later, Pickering decided to sell the entire operation to Cipriani. Between what Cipriani was able to raise and subtracting Pickering's enormous unpaid bar tab from the sum, they reached an agreement and the bar was Cipriani's. He chose to continue to call it Harry's.

The war years of 1939 to 1945 were difficult ones for Cipriani. First, now that England and Italy were at war, the fascist Italian government forced Cipriani to change the name of the bar to Bar Arrigo (Italian for "Harry"). Later, the bar was confiscated by the Italian navy and used as a mess hall. When the Allied forces arrived in the city, the U.S. commander summoned Cipriani and demanded that Harry's Bar be reopened.

Harry's Gifts to the World

Besides being a great bar and restaurant, Harry's Bar has given some unique gastronomical gifts to the world. The Bellini, a cocktail combining white peach juice and sparkling Italian wine, was an invention of Giuseppe Cipriani. Cipriani  also invented the bar's signature dish, Beef Carpaccio, a treat of thin slices of rare filet mignon layered with a white cream sauce, when one of his regular customers complained that her doctor had just put her on a restrictive diet of no cooked meats. The last invention of Harry's, the Montgomery Martini, is owed not to Cipriani, but to his most famous patron, Ernest Hemingway. Hemingway named the cocktail for its distinctive 15:1 ratio of gin to vermouth, the same ratio he said famed General Montgomery preferred when engaging the enemy.

Harry's has been open ever since and it quickly became a watering hole for the rich and famous. Noted guests have included Humphrey Bogart and Lauren Bacall, Orson Welles, Sinclair Lewis, Charlie Chaplin, Aristotle Onasis, Truman Capote and Woody Allen to name a few. Undoubtedly, the most famous patron at Harry's was Ernest Hemingway, who practically lived there from 1949 to 1950. At the time, Hemingway was working on *Across the River and into the Trees* and he immortalised Harry's Bar in some of his scenes:

"There was no one in Harry's except some early morning drinkers that the Colonel didn't know and two men that were doing business at the back of the bar."

"There were hours at Harry's when it filled with the people that you knew, with the same rushing regularity as the tide coming in at Mont St. Michel. Except, the Colonel thought, the hours for the tides change each day with the moon and the hours at Harry's are as the Greenwich Meridian, or the standard meter in Paris or the good opinion the French military hold of themselves."

Hemingway and the other celebrities certainly contributed to the lasting success of Harry's Bar but the real secret to its success, according to Giuseppe (in the memoirs by his son and current proprietor Arrigo), is that there is no secret except that anyone who visits Harry's will always find three things: quality, a smile and simplicity. How true.

Itinerant Horses

Horses of St. Mark's, St. Mark's Basilica

A series of splendid sculptures survives for 20 centuries and becomes a prized trophy, but for more than one conqueror.

Venice loves its symbols—the lions, the gondolas, the masks of Carnival—but near the top of that list are a squad of four ancient bronze horses, which somehow came to symbolise the power of a seafaring republic. Sitting atop a 1000-year-old basilica, the horses of St. Mark's do look a bit out of place. Yet there they are, bearing testament to conquests long ago. The origin of the horses is up for question by most scholars but they are, without doubt, some of the rarest bronze sculptures that survive to this day. This is a truly amazing feat when you consider their travels.

The horses were originally part of a sculpture of a four-horse chariot team called a quadriga, which may have been atop the Arch of Trajan in Rome (now destroyed). These chariot-team sculptures were quite common in the Roman world but the horses of St. Mark's are the only team of four that survives to the present day. From Rome, the quadriga was taken to Constantinople, probably by Constantine himself, where they adorned the hippodrome racetrack. They stayed in Constantinople for over eight centuries until the Venetians arrived in 1204.

The Crusades of the 12th century had been good for Venice; the city had been a major provider of ships, arms and material. The fourth Crusade at the dawn of the 13th century proved to be an even greater boon for the city. In 1202, the armies of the fourth Crusade assembled in Venice to gather provisions for their quest. The necessary funds from Germany to pay for the thousands of men and horses and the ships to carry them were delayed so Doge Enrico Dandolo agreed to the provisions, provided that the expedition first recaptured the city of Zara, a Venetian city recently lost to the Hungarians. This was done but, during the six months that it took to conquer Zara, a political crisis took place in Constantinople, in which two rivals vied for succession to the throne. The expedition stopped at Constantinople to throw its might to the side Venice favoured (for trading purposes). After failed diplomacy, the Crusaders, led by Doge Dandolo (who was 85 and completely blind), took the city by force and plundered it. The four horses at the hippodrome formed part of the bounty and were shipped back to Venice.

The horses were first taken to the Arsenale to undergo partial restoration and to repair any damage done during their removal and transportation from Constantinople. It is not known how long this work took but the horses stayed in the shipyard for 50 years before being moved to the basilica. It is quite likely that those working in the Arsenale looked at the four horses more for their base metals than for their historical significance. Thankfully, the horses escaped the foundry furnace and were in place above the central arch in the façade of St. Mark's by 1265.

Only in Venice, where East meets West, where Byzantium met Rome, where traders from all over the Mediterranean and Europe mingled together, will you find horses atop a church.

Once in place atop the church, they quickly became a landmark of the city as noted by many in the Middle Ages. Petrarch described the horses in a letter dated 1364 as "those four bronze and gild horses, the work of some ancient and famous artist unknown to us, stand as if alive, seeming to neigh from on high and paw with their hooves." Later, in 1379, Pietro Doria, the Genoese commander who strove to capture Venice, threatened to "bridle those unreined horses that stand on St. Mark's."

For the next 500 years, the horses stood atop the basilica as an enduring symbol of the city's power. By the end of the 18th century, however, the French were approaching and Venice's power was all but gone. Napoleon reached Venice in the autumn of 1797 and forced the city into submission. Napoleon's arrival marked the end of the Venetian republic. He sold Venice's territories to Vienna and plundered the city's finest treasures for transport back to France. The horses of St. Mark's were at the top of his list. They were removed from the basilica in December 1797 amid a solemn ceremony in the piazza. The people of Venice were heartbroken with the loss of their beloved horses, as captured by resident Lord Byron in *Childe Harold's Pilgrimage*:

"Before St. Mark still glow his steeds of brass,

Their gilded collars glittering in the sun,

But is not Doria's menace come to pass?

Are they not bridled? Venice, lost and won,

Her thirteen hundred years of freedom done,

Sinks like a sea-weed into whence she rose!"

The horses went to Paris, where they were to stay for the next 18 years. Their return was negotiated after Napoleon was defeated at Waterloo. The horses were returned to Venice in December 1815. They were floated from the mainland on a large raft amid a 21-gun salute and were hoisted back in place amid a throng of wildly cheering Venetians.

The horses were moved again in 1915, this time to Rome, which was further away from the trenches of World War I. During World

War II, the horses were again removed from the basilica and were placed in the basement of the Doge's Palace for safety. The horses were separated (perhaps for the first time in their existence) in 1980 as a single horse was sent as part of an exhibition to London and New York. Upon their reunification, the horses were not returned to their centuries-old position atop the basilica. Instead, they were restored and placed inside the basilica to protect them, this time, from the elements. And the horses that now stand proudly in the central arch of the basilica's façade? They are fibreglass copies of the originals.

The Wrong Heads?

People throughout history have commented about the odd positioning of the heads of the horses. They noted specifically that the two sets of horses seem to have their heads set inwards whereas a more standard set of four horses would have their heads facing outwards. It is known that the heads were removed from the bodies to make transportation easier from Constantinople. Many have speculated that the heads were put back on incorrectly upon arrival in Venice and have been left that way ever since.

Lord Byron's Venice

Palazzo Mocenigo

A famous English lord flees sexual scandal in his native land and makes his mark in the 'sea-Sodom' of 19th-century Venice.

Reading about Byron's life, it seems almost inevitable that he would travel to Venice. A young, charismatic and handsome nobleman with an enormous sexual appetite for both women and men, he was a poor fit for 19th-century England. In 1816, at age 28, he fled England under mounting debts, a failed marriage and increasing accusations of homosexuality and fostering an incestuous relationship with his half-sister. His destination—legendary Venice, a place he called the greenest island of his imagination. It was a perfect choice for the author, adventurer and amorist. The architecture and history of the city fed his fertile mind and were the seed for a handful of his written works. The women of Venice, dark, passionate and flirtatious, were to feed other things fertile.

Byron immediately fell in love with Venice as he stated in a letter to his friend Thomas Moore: "It [Venice] has not disappointed me, though its evident decay would, perhaps, have that effect upon others. But I have been familiar with ruins too long to dislike desolation. Besides, I have fallen in love, which, next to falling into the canal, (which would have been no use as I can swim) is the best or the worst thing I could do. I have got some extremely good apartments in the house of a 'Merchant of Venice', who is a good deal occupied with business, and has a wife in her twenty-second year."

Marianna, the merchant's wife, was Byron's first Venetian love. "Her spouse," he wrote in a letter to his half-sister, "is a very good kind of man who occupies himself elsewhere and (Marianna) does not plague me and I verily believe we are one of the happiest unlawful couples this side of the Alps." Such open infidelity was commonplace in Venice at the time as Byron continued: "Indeed everyone is [loose], so much so that a lady with only one lover is not reckoned to have overstepped the modesty of marriage—that being a regular thing. Some have two, three, and so on to twenty, beyond which they don't account…The husbands of course belong to any body's wives—but their own."

Byron continued his liaison with Marianna but he was quick to learn the drawbacks of a hot-tempered Latin love. One evening during Carnival, Byron was visited by Marianna's 19-year-old sister-in-law. A few moments later, Marianna entered, quickly curtsied to the English lord, grabbed her sister-in-law by the hair and gave her sixteen slaps, which Byron wrote "made your ear ache only to hear the echo." The young girl escaped and Marianna subsequently fainted. Byron was further troubled when Marianna's husband arrived, demanding to know what had happened. Byron captured the moment in a letter to Moore: "You need not be alarmed—jealousy is not the order of the day in Venice, and daggers are out of fashion; while duels, on love matters, are unknown—at least with the husbands." It was not the last of such squabbles, which often drove Byron from his home. In fact, he once spent the night in a gondola on the lagoon in order to gain peace.

Lame Lord

A little-known fact about Lord Byron is that he was born with a clubbed foot. While he did get the benefit of an orthopaedic shoe to address the problem as a child, the problem affected him until the end of his days. He was terribly self-conscious of his uneven gait, even avoiding St. Mark's Square, which he claims to have never seen in his three years in Venice, lest he be seen limping across it.

Although Byron enjoyed many, many women in Venice, he had two great loves there. The first was Marianna. The second, Margarita Cogni, a baker's wife. Margarita was from a lower class in Venice but her unbending pride more than accounted for her lower position in society. Both women were extremely possessive of Byron and were often at loggerheads. In one instance, Byron's new interest berated Marianna: "You are his woman and I am his woman; your husband is a cuckold and so is mine. What right have you to approach me? If he prefers what is mine to what is yours, is it my fault? Don't think you can speak to me like this just because you are rich." In the end, they decided they would share him, along with many others. In the end, Byron had his fill of Margarita as well, with explosive results. When he tired of her, she flew into a rage and stabbed him with a kitchen knife before throwing herself into the Grand Canal.

It was about this time that Byron cemented his expatriate lifestyle. He sold his family estate in England and rented the furnished Palazzo Mocenigo on the Grand Canal for £200 a year. He hired fourteen servants and brought his valet from England. He lived alone in the large palazzo except for his menagerie of pets—a fox, a wolf, two large mastiffs, two monkeys and a large collection of pheasants—which occupied the entire first floor.

By this time, Byron had acquired quite a reputation in the city. In a time of excess, he had more lovers than most men could have dreamed of. He never rose before midday and often worked at his pen, or at his lovers, until sunrise. Byron, an accomplished swimmer, also drew the attention of Venetians because of his curious habit of swimming back to the Palazzo Mocenigo, fully clothed, after a night of amorous adventures. He even got into the habit of carrying a torch in one hand so as not to get run down by passing gondoliers.

An Adept Swimmer

Lord Byron was renowned for his swimming ability, having swum the Bosporus Strait in Turkey. In the summer of 1818, he won a swimming contest from the Lido to the Doge's Palace. Not only did he win by more than half a kilometre, he continued past the palace and swam the length of the Grand Canal, totalling nearly four hours in the water without resting. He later wrote to his friend John Hobhouse that he "could not have been too fatigued, having had a woman in the forenoon and taking another in the evening at ten o'clock."

Palazzo Mocenigo—the palazzo that Lord Byron called home during his time in Venice.

Nineteenth-century Venice and the Palazzo Mocenigo proved to be the perfect playground for Byron, where he could fulfil desires deemed appalling back in England. Byron's contemporary and friend poet Percy Shelley captured his sentiments on the situation in a letter to novelist Thomas Love Peacock: "Well, Lord Byron is familiar with the lowest class of these women, the people his gondoliers pick up in the streets. He allows fathers and mothers to bargain with him for their daughters and though this is common enough in Italy, yet for an Englishman to encourage such sickening vice is a melancholy thing…He says he disapproves, but he endures."

Life Imitating Art

Byron put his life experiences down in writing as it was during his stay in Venice that he began his famous work *Don Juan*.

The lusty lord once bragged to a friend that he had bedded 200 women in as many nights. But even gluttons can become tired of the table. He wrote the following, *So We'll Go No More A Roving*, after throwing himself into the festivities of Carnival.

"So we'll go no more a roving
So late into the night,
Though the heart be still as loving,
And the moon be still as bright.

"For the sword outwears its sheath,
And the soul wears out the breast,
And the heart must pause to breathe,
And Love itself have rest.

"Though the night was made for loving,
And the day returns too soon,
Yet, we'll go no more a roving
By the light of the moon."

Byron justified his excesses in a letter to his friend John Hobhouse: "I shall not live long, and for that reason I must live while I can…for the night cometh." A fitting epitaph indeed. Byron left Venice and the Palazzo Mocenigo in 1819 and lived only a few more years, dying at the age of 36.

Losing One's Head

Veiled portrait of Marin Falier in the Ballot Chamber, Doge's Palace

A hotheaded elder statesman is elected Doge of Venice but his quick temper causes him to lose his head.

The early 14th century was filled with difficulties for Venice. In 1309, Venice fought against the pope for control of the city of Ferrara and lost (getting the whole of Venice excommunicated from the Church in the process). The next year, the republic barely escaped a coup attempt. During this time, the city's ongoing conflict with Genoa was also progressing poorly, Then in 1348, the plague struck, killing an estimated 600 people a day. Six years later, Venice's beloved Doge Andrea Dandolo died an untimely death. The final insult was to come the following year when the newly elected Doge, Marin Falier, knelt beneath the executioner's blade in disgrace.

Andrea Dandolo was an exceptionally gifted man. He was appointed the medieval equivalent of mayor to the city of Trieste as a youth. He was a learned scholar, who wrote two volumes of the history of the Venetian republic (up to his day) in Latin, and served as a military commander and financial officer. In 1342, when Doge Bartolomeo Gradenigo died, Dandolo was the unanimous choice for succession despite the incredible fact that he had not yet reached the age of 40 (most doges were in their seventies). Dandolo's youth and vigour breathed new life into Venice and Venetian politics and he was much beloved by the younger nobility of the city.

After mourning Dandolo's untimely passing at the age of 47, the city settled on a successor. Marin Falier seemed a perfect choice for the dogeship. He came from one of Venice's oldest families and had spent over 40 years in public service. He had served as mayor of Padua, Treviso and Chioggia, as a naval commander and had even sat on the secretive and powerful Council of Ten, which had been set up to thwart the power of individuals and families after the Querini-Tiepolo coup plot of 1310. At the time of Dandolo's death, Falier was serving as the Venetian ambassador to the papal court. He was 76 years old. To the elders in Venetian politics, Falier seemed a natural choice. After all, the dogeship was the culminating reward for a lifetime of service to the republic. To its younger members, however, Falier seemed a dinosaur and a step back to the old status quo.

Falier, for all his gifts and his service to the republic, had a fatal flaw—a short temper. It was this temper that would quickly bring the new Doge to his end.

Marin Falier's dogeship was troubled from the very beginning. He arrived in Venice in October 1354 in a fog so thick that the *Bucintoro*, the lavishly decorated ship used only by the Doge, could not approach the Doge's Palace. Instead, he had to go ashore in a small utility boat. Even then, the boat could only be docked at the edge of St. Mark's Square, meaning that Falier had to go ashore between the square's two columns. Having to do so even today is considered a very bad omen as this was the traditional place of execution.

After the election ceremonies, Doge Falier hosted a banquet for the city's noble and patrician families in the Doge's Palace, during which he was set inexorably on the path to his ruin. During the banquet, a young nobleman got drunk and made unseemly advances towards one of the Doge's wife's female attendants. The man was escorted out of the banquet but managed to slip his escort long enough to scrawl an insulting stanza suggesting that Falier was a cuckold on the Doge's throne:

"Marin Falier has a wife that is fair,

[but] he has to keep her while other men lay her."

Falier was furious to say the least and demanded that the perpetrator be brought to justice. The man was apprehended and stood before a tribunal. Falier was expecting the young man's head but instead the tribunal let the man go with a very light censure. Consequently, Falier became further enraged as he considered the light judgment to be the court's tacit approval for what the young man had done. The disdain the young Venetian aristocrats felt for Falier was soon to be a mere fraction of the disdain that he felt for them.

Meanwhile, two other respected citizens drew up complaints that they had been insulted and accosted by young Venetian nobles. One was a naval commander, the other was Stefano Ghiazza, the director of the Arsenale, Venice's famous shipyard. In Falier's mind, something had to be done about these upstarts. When he overhead Ghiazza saying of his assailants that "Dangerous beasts must be tied up; if they cannot be controlled they must be destroyed", he knew that Ghiazza would be the perfect man to help put these youngsters in their place. As director of the Arsenale, Ghiazza had control over some 5000 men who could take up arms at a moment's notice, men who were traditionally loyal to the Doge and frequently used as his bodyguards. The Doge asked for help and Ghiazza was only too happy to oblige.

The plot was to take place on 15 April. That evening, a rumour was to be circulated around the city of an impending Genoese fleet (a very real threat at the time). This false threat would undoubtedly draw all of the city's aristocracy, both old and young, to St. Mark's Square, where the armed workers of the Arsenale would be waiting to cut down the young nobility in defence of the Doge. Doge Marin Falier would then be declared the prince of Venice to public acclaim.

Unfortunately for the Doge and his accomplices, the plot was uncovered when one of the conspirators mentioned to a friend to stay at home on that particular night. The man went immediately to the Doge to relay his concern but Doge Falier dismissed the man and his warning too quickly, tipping off his own involvement. So the man then went to the Council of Ten with his concerns and it listened.

The Council quickly determined the threat to be real and made ready a militia of loyal men from all parts of the city. On the morning of the 15th, the Council and its militia began arresting the plotters. These men were summarily hanged from the palace windows overlooking St.

Mark's Square. Doge Falier was the last to be arrested. He did not deny the charges and provided a full confession to the Council. After two days of deliberation, the Ten made their decision. On the morning of 17 April, 76-year-old Marin Falier was escorted from his apartment to the marble staircase that opened onto the palace courtyard. A chopping block lay at the top of the stairs. In a short speech, Falier asked for the republic's forgiveness for his crime, then kneeled down and laid his head on the block. The executioner severed the old man's head with a single stroke. His headless body was then displayed to the public before being buried in an unmarked grave.

A Grim Reminder

After Marin Falier's execution, the Doge was always followed by a man carrying a heavy sword during all formal processions. This was to act as a reminder of what befell the treachery of Falier, a tradition that continued for over 400 years.

The members of the Council of Ten could not bring themselves to enter the Doge's name on the list of those condemned in the plot, leaving instead a blank entry followed by the words *non scribatur*, meaning "let it not be written". Ten years later, Doge Falier's portrait was permanently removed from the succession of portraits in the Ballot Chamber. It was painted over with a faux black velvet veil, still seen today, with the inscription: *Hic est locus Marini Faledri decapitati pro criminibus* (Here is the place of Marin Falier, beheaded for his crimes).

Marin Falier's veiled portrait hangs in the Sala Maggiore in the Doge's Palace. When his grave was opened in the 19th century, it was found to contain a skeleton with the skull placed between the knees.

Napoleon Returns

Statue of Napoleon, Napoleonic Wing, Museo Correr

Two hundred years after conquering Venice, a lost statue of Napoleon is found and returned to the city. Today, he stands in a museum built on his own orders, an unwelcome guest in the city he plundered two centuries earlier.

Venice was a proud city and the Venetians a proud people. And this pride was not unfounded. The city had survived as a republic for nearly 1300 years. It had defended itself against all enemies and its city had remained inviolate. By the 1700s, however, Venice was in a state of decline. Economically, it was now just one of many trading centres in the Mediterranean. Militarily, Britannia now ruled the waves, not the Venetians. Morally, Venice had slid into a malaise of gambling, excess and the concupiscence of Casanova and his contemporaries. But if the city was on its road to decline, one man would radically hasten the process.

As a young officer in the French army, Napoleon Bonaparte would no doubt have heard tales about Venice: its water streets and sea girth, its haughty Doge, its gilded riches, its Inquisition, its notorious prisons, its corrupt aristocrats, its prideful winged lion. As commander-in-chief of the French army, he would have the chance to see them in person.

Throughout 1796 to 1797, Napoleon staged a masterful campaign across northern Italy. One by one the cities fell: Milan, Bergamo, Verona, Padua. Napoleon and his forces marched ever closer to Venice. Venice, with an army much smaller than that of the French, professed its neutrality. The Venetians might well have escaped the Corsican's wrath had two events not occurred. Citizens of the city of Verona, still technically a Venetian territory though occupied by French forces, rose up against their occupiers and massacred 400 wounded French soldiers in the city hospital. Shortly thereafter, a Venetian battery on the Lido fired on a French patrol vessel. Napoleon set his sights squarely on Venice and let the city know it. In communiqués to the Venetian Senate, he wrote: "I will have no more Inquisition, I will have no more Senate; I shall be an Attila to the state of Venice." On 9 May, he declared war on Venice, claiming he would make the winged lion of St. Mark lick the dust.

It did not take long. The lagoon, which had protected the city and its residents so many times before, could not protect against the French cannons. Three days later, the Senate convened to review Napoleon's demands. The vote was 512 to 20 for surrender with 5 abstentions. Lodovico Manin, Venice's 120th and final Doge, turned to his valet upon hearing the vote, handed him the linen cap worn under the ducal crown and said, "Take this, I shall not be needing it again." The Venetian republic was finished without a shot being fired. Napoleon did not even enter the city but his troops did.

The French army's plunder of Venice ranks as one of the most complete in history. They removed the winged lion and the bronze horses from St. Mark's, ships and material from the Arsenale, the entire flotilla, gold, jewels, paintings and manuscripts. It is estimated that of all the artistic treasures that Venice had amassed in her 1300 years, only 4% still remains in the city today.

Good Deeds

For all his faults, of which there are many according to most Venetians, Napoleon did carry out some good deeds. These included opening up the Jewish Ghetto, which had been guarded as a virtual prison for close to 500 years, and the creation of public gardens, namely the *giardini pubblici* in the *sestiere* of Castello.

Napoleon eventually travelled to Venice for a mere ten-day visit in 1807, but those ten days left a lasting impression on the city. Napoleon, then a self-proclaimed French emperor, gave sweeping demands for public improvement (at least as he saw it). Religious reform was at the top of his list. Fifty-nine monasteries and convents were closed and somewhere between fifty and seventy-five churches were either destroyed or converted to other, usually French military, uses. Churches were converted to gymnasiums, prisons, hotels and even taverns. One famous church, San Geminiano on St. Mark's Square, was torn down to make room for a grand ballroom (currently the Napoleonic Wing of the Museo Correr), which he would never return to use.

Modern Piazza

Napoleon uttered the famous quote that St. Mark's Square was "the finest drawing room in Europe." His heavy-handed 'urban renewal' has much to do with the modern look of the square.

Napoleon also mandated that Venice should be a tax-free port, a decree well received by local traders who commissioned a large statue to the emperor. Unveiled in St. Mark's Square in 1811, the statue was tastefully moved across the Grand Canal to the island of San Giorgio Maggiore after Napoleon was defeated at Waterloo.

The statue went missing in the 19th century, only to turn up for auction at Sotheby's in New York in 2002. It was purchased by a French association dedicated to Venetian preservation and shipped back to Venice to be housed in the Napoleonic wing of the Museo Correr. Not all were happy to see him return. A group of Venetians held a mock trial for the returning emperor, holding him to account for the destruction he wrought upon the city 200 years earlier.

Housed in the Napoleonic wing of the Museo Correr, this marble statue of Napoleon was sculpted by Venetian Domenico Banti in 1811.

The Honest Courtesan

Church of San Moise, Campo San Moise

*An exceptional call girl rises through the ranks of
Venetian society to mingle with (and serve) the city's
male elite and the crowns of Europe.*

Venice has been described in many ways: *la serenissima* (the most serene), the Jewel of the Adriatic, a maritime power, the home of St. Mark, a medieval and Renaissance trading mecca, the gateway to the East. One thing that often gets overlooked about Venice is that it was a port city. And like all port cities of the era, Venice, too, had its share of 'professional' ladies.

The 16th-century Venetian chronicler Marin Sanudo put the number of Venetian prostitutes at over 11,000, an incredible number when you consider that the population in the lagoon at that time was an estimated 100,000. This carnal trade was tolerated in Renaissance Venice as less a crime in itself than curbing more violent crimes born out of unsatisfied desire. These labourers for Venus came from and serviced all levels of society, from lowly deck hands to visiting royalty.

The elite of these women, the *cortigiane oneste*, or honest courtesans, were accepted into Venetian high society. These ladies were well educated, literate (and often published authors), accomplished musicians and conversationalists. They attended balls, pageants, parties, state functions and even attended Mass regularly. Some of them even came from noted and even noble Venetian families. They were the most famous, and in some cases the most infamous, women of their day. The most famous of these Venetian courtesans was Veronica Franco.

Veronica was born to the patrician, bourgeois Franco family in 1546. No details exist on the fate of the Franco family in the mid-16th century, but her mother Paola, though now married and with a family, had once been a Venetian courtesan. By her 17th birthday, Veronica had followed her mother into the world's oldest profession.

Although Veronica eventually became the most well-known woman of her time, and one of the highest paid for her favours, her start was not so spectacular. In 1564, a book was published (anonymously) in Venice which detailed the names of all the Venetian courtesans (215 in total), their addresses and their fees. Veronica was listed in the book. Her fee was 2 scudi; the lowest fee in the book was 1 scudo.

By the time she was 28, her fortunes had changed dramatically. A letter from an admirer of Veronica's complained about the 50 scudi she charged. But it was a visit to Venice by King Henri III of France that cemented Veronica's place as the queen of Venetian courtesans.

Venice delighted the 22-year-old king of France with banquets, parades and performances. Even glass blowers from Murano came to the city to give exhibitions of their arts. He was also made an honorary member of the Senate. And for his personal pleasure, he reviewed an album of miniature portraits of the city's courtesans and chose Veronica Franco. Undoubtedly, the liaison was supposed to have been a secret one but soon the whole island was abuzz with details of the intrigue. It was then that Veronica garnered the unofficial title of "Ornament of the City".

When she published her book of poems, *Terze rime*, to some acclaim the next year, her celebrity status was near its zenith. With no end to her list of possible suitors, Veronica could afford to be choosy with her affections. Indeed, she spurned many rich and powerful men because they did not please her. These rejections must have stung badly for the men she turned away but also revealed a deeper feeling of superiority that she now had over her clientele. In many men's minds, a woman for sale should be for sale to anyone. Veronica's discriminating tastes did not sit well with many in Venice and it was not long before slander filled the air.

One spurned suitor turned to his pen and ink well and produced a satirical poem about her. Veronica countered with a publicly circulated letter in which she promised that his slanders would come back to him. She concluded the letter by expressing: "I could not believe that it [the poem] was yours, as it was so imperfect a work and so full of mistakes."

The most painful attack, however, came from Maffio Venier, a nephew of Veronica's main patron Domenico Venier, in the form of a poem titled *Veronica, ver unica puttana* (*Veronica, truly unique whore*) in which he disparaged her terribly. She again responded with a public letter: "So ready now paper and ink and tell me without delay which weapons I must wield in combat. You have nowhere to run from me, because I am prepared for any test and impatiently wait to begin. You may choose everyday parlance or whichever idiom you please, for I am skilled in them all." If quality of poetry and prose is any gauge, Maffio was outmatched.

Her notoriety also drew the attention of the Venetian Inquisition in 1580, the same year her letters were published. She was charged with sorcery and for not attending Mass. There was no evidence of the first charge. She defended herself successfully against the second charge by saying that she had been ill and concluded with the tongue-in-cheek statement that she had been confined to her bed for the past four months.

Towards the end of her short life, there is evidence that she had a change of heart about her chosen profession. In one of her later letters, she chastises a woman for allowing her daughter to become a courtesan, warning her that she would "kill in one blow not only a soul but also your own honor and that of your daughter."

Describing the life of a courtesan, she penned: "You can do nothing worse in this life… than to force the body into such servitude…To give oneself in prey to so many, to risk being despoiled, robbed or killed…and also the danger of infectious diseases. To eat with someone else's mouth, to sleep with the eyes of others, to move as someone else desires, and to risk the shipwreck of your faculties and your life—what could be worse?"

Veronica Franco's tomb lies in the Church of San Moise. During her lifetime, she was accepted as a literary peer by many academics of the day including Domenico Venier.

In a final attempt to rehabilitate herself, she decreed in her will that her entire surplus should go towards the dowry of two worthy maidens who did not have a dowry of their own. She stressed that if two prostitutes could be found who were willing to abandon their wicked life and marry, they were to be selected before the two maidens. She was buried in the Church of San Moise in 1591.

The Lion's Mouth

Bocca di Leone, outside the Sala della Bussola, Doge's Palace

A secretive government council installs anonymous letterboxes around the city for Venetians to inform on formative coups and plots but the system quickly gets abused as citizens denounce one another for political or financial gain. One such denunciation eventually drives a popular Doge and his family to ruin.

Venice in the 14th and 15th centuries was an imbroglio of intrigue. Noble families spied on one another for political and financial gain. The underclass struggled to topple the elite. Youth chided the older patricians of the city while older patricians plotted against the younger generation.

In 1310, the republic narrowly escaped a coup attempt in which a handful of powerful families made a play for ultimate power against the state. In response, the Senate and Doge moved to strengthen their control over the city by creating the secretive Council of Ten, a shadowy group of ten senior officials. The Council of Ten was authorised to hold secret trials and assessed internal threats to the city as gathered by their secret police, paid spies and informants and through anonymous denunciations dropped into one of a series of

Only a few bocce di leone *survive to this day, including this one outside the Sala della Bussola in the Doge's Palace.*

public letterboxes named the *bocce di leone*, the lions' mouths. These letterboxes were designed as a way for upstanding citizens to denounce criminals and malefactors to the authorities. However, as the power of the Council of Ten grew, so too did the potential for abuse of the bocce di leone. In one interesting case, the bocce di leone both saved and destroyed a powerful family, the family of Doge Francesco Foscari.

Francesco Foscari was elected Doge in 1423 after the death of Doge Tommaso Mocenigo. Mocenigo on his deathbed had warned the Senate not to elect Foscari on the grounds that he would plunge the republic into a series of costly conflicts. Venice ignored the dying Doge's advice and elected Foscari, who promptly went to war. Over the next decade, the republic gained territory on the mainland in northern Italy but floundered financially at home as the state treasury was virtually empty due to the military campaigns. Several banks failed and many trading houses closed. Personal bankruptcies of established noble families, once unheard of, were now commonplace. Foscari was making enemies, powerful enemies.

In 1430, an attempt was made on Foscari's life. Three years later, a conspiracy of young nobles against the Doge was uncovered, presumably by denunciation through the bocce di leone, and subsequently quashed. The family of Pietro Loredan, the man who Foscari had narrowly, and some report underhandedly, defeated for the dogeship, would prove to be another dangerous enemy. However, the biggest hindrance to Francesco Foscari's rule came from Jacopo, his only surviving son.

Jacopo Foscari, by all accounts, was a frivolous and irresponsible young man who advanced only so far as he did with his father's assistance. Jacopo was betrothed to a lady of the Loredans in an attempt to heal the rift between the two families. The marriage was an unhappy one and ended quickly. The Foscari and the Loredans were now completely at odds and the Loredan family would soon have the opportunity for vengeance.

In 1445, Jacopo, heavily in debt, was accused of accepting bribes and gifts from citizens and even foreign princes who wished to influence the Doge in one direction or another. This was considered a serious offence. The Council of Ten, including one member of the Loredan family—Francesco, convened to review the evidence and immediately called for Jacopo's arrest. It was too late; Jacopo had already fled the city. The trial continued in Jacopo's absence and damning evidence was found in his home. Francesco Loredan led the prosecution and Jacopo was sentenced in absentia to lifelong exile from Venice to an island in Peloponnesus. The Council commuted this sentence two years later after an emotional appeal by Jacopo's father, the Doge. The Council ruled: "considering the need in these difficult times that our Doge should be free of frets and worry for the greater service to the Republic." Jacopo returned to Venice in 1447.

All seemed well for the two Foscari until the autumn of 1450 when Ermolao Donato, a distinguished senator and member of the Council of Ten that had sentenced Jacopo five years earlier, was assassinated by an unknown assailant. Jacopo Foscari was not suspected in the crime until someone slipped an anonymous denunciation into one of the bocce di leone naming him as Donato's killer. Revenge was given as the motive.

Twain's Take

Mark Twain wrote of the lions' mouths of Venice in his travel work *Innocents Abroad*. "These were the terrible Lions' Mouths. ... these were the throats down which went the anonymous accusation thrust in secretly in the dead of night by an enemy, that doomed many an innocent man to walk the Bridge of Sighs and descend into the dungeon which none entered and hoped to see the sun again."

Jacopo was promptly arrested (before he had the opportunity to flee again) and was brought to stand before the Ten. The Council could not gain a confession from young Jacopo, even after he was tortured. It mattered not. He was sentenced again to lifelong exile from Venice, this time to Crete.

Things might have ended there but for Jacopo's foolishness. In 1456, the Council of Ten discovered that Jacopo had been in secret correspondence with Venice's mortal enemy, the sultan of Turkey, in order to arrange transport off the Cretan island. This was a treasonable offence. He was brought back to Venice in chains to stand once again before the Ten, this time hosted by another Loredan, Jacopo. Torture was not necessary this time as Jacopo Foscari confessed freely to the correspondence. Jacopo Loredan suggested the young Foscari be executed between the columns on St. Mark's Square but was overruled by the other nine members. Instead, they decided to send Foscari back to Crete, this time to be imprisoned. Doge Francesco Foscari was allowed to visit his son in prison before his departure, a meeting during which the son implored his father to use his powers to influence the Council and pardon him. Much to his credit, the Doge advised his son to obey the will of the republic and return to Crete. Six months later, word reached Venice that Jacopo Foscari was dead.

Francesco Foscari was devastated at the loss of his last surviving child and he withdrew from his duties and sank into a deep depression. The final insult came when the Council of Ten, now led by Jacopo Loredan, forcibly removed 84-year-old Doge Foscari from his office in a ceremony devoid of the respect due to someone in his position. Eight days later, Francesco Foscari died.

A Story for the Stage

The tragedy of Francisco and Jacopo Foscari was immortalised, nearly 400 years later, by Lord Byron who penned his play *The Two Foscari* while living in Venice. This play later became the basis for Verdi's opera of the same name.

Nearly 700 years after their first use, the bocce di leone can still be found in some corners of the city. One wonders if letters are still slipped into the holes and if a city official still reads them.

Which Ones Survive?

At their height, dozens of denunciation boxes were dotted around the city. Different bocce di leone were used to report different grievances or violations, including tax evasion, street repair, threats to the state, poor sanitation and crimes. In 1797, Napoleon ordered their withdrawal and destruction as part of his campaign to dismantle the apparatus of the Venetian republic. As a result, only a few of the bocce di leone survive to this day.

126

The Master of the House, Reincarnated

Campanile, St. Mark's Square

One of Venice's signature landmarks, a 1000-year-old tower, unexpectedly falls into a heap of rubble—only to be rebuilt exactly as it was and exactly where it was.

Standing as the tallest structure in all of the Venetian lagoon, the Campanile di San Marco, along with St. Mark's Basilica and the Rialto Bridge, is one of Venice's signature landmarks. In its long history overlooking the comings and goings of Venice, it has seen it all, which is why the Venetians refer to the tower as the "Master of the House".

Construction of the tower first began in 888 and was completed nearly 300 years

Standing tall, the Campanile in St. Mark's Square.

later. There are no accounts as to why it took so long to build. It was rebuilt during the Renaissance in the form we see today. Its original function was to serve as a guard tower over the dock at the edge of the square but it has had a number of uses since then.

In the 1300s, cannons were placed in the belfry when Venice's arch-rival, the Genoese, threatened to invade. In the Middle Ages, prisoners were placed in an iron cage and dangled outside from the belfry for all the city to see.

The Bell Tolls for Thee

There are five separate bells in the belfry of the Campanile and while not all are tolled today, each had a distinct meaning to Venetians past. The largest of the bells, Marangona, was sounded to signal the beginning and end of the working day. The bell called Nona was rung to mark midday while the Mezza Terza announced Senate meetings and the Trottiera called nobles to the Doge's Palace. The smallest bell, known as the Renghiera or Maleficio, was rung to announce the execution of a prisoner.

Polished bronze panels were then added to the outside of the belfry in the 1500s. These panels acted as a kind of daytime lighthouse as the reflected Sun could be seen by sailors approaching from the Adriatic. Venice's Master of the House played host to a master of a different type when Galileo came calling.

Galileo—scientist, inventor, academic, philosopher—travelled to the region of Venice in 1592 and gained a contract to fill the prestigious mathematics chair at the nearby University of Padua, beating another great mind, Giordano Bruno, for the job. Galileo was a regular visitor to Venice and, with the help of world-class glass workers on the nearby island of Murano, completed one of his most famous works there.

Galileo and the Arsenale

Whenever Galileo visited Venice, he made regular trips to the city's famous military shipyard, the Arsenale. For the better part of his life, Galileo worked on theories of mechanics and motion, and the heavy and military industries of the Arsenale proved to be a great workshop for him. There, he assisted the designers of warships with ship design and improved oar techniques and cannon ballistics.

Contrary to popular belief, Galileo did not invent the telescope; it was already well known throughout Europe. However, he did perfect the design. The original telescope design at the beginning of the 1600s magnified objects to three times their size. In 1609, Galileo perfected the telescope to such an extent that objects could be magnified up to eight times. In the same year, he and Doge Leonardo Dona climbed to the top of the Campanile where Galileo demonstrated the device that made objects on the distant mainland look as though they were only a stone's throw from the piazza. Doge Dona was duly impressed and immediately placed an order for the improved telescope (for use on warships). He also immediately doubled Galileo's salary at the university.

The Master of the House has truly witnessed history in the making in its time: Venice's rise to become a world sea power, Doges executed, Casanova's escape, Lord Byron swimming in the Grand Canal, Napoleon and the end of the republic and Austrian occupation. Yet even this wizened old veteran could not have foreseen what lay in store for it at the dawn of the 20th century.

Few people visiting Venice today realise that the Campanile towering over the piazza is a reincarnation of the original, which collapsed on 14 July 1902. An American architect visiting at the time of the collapse described the event, as quoted in *Winters of Content*:

"Workmen had been repointing the Campanile, and had discovered a bad crack starting from the crown of the second arched window on the corner towards St. Mark's, and extending through the sixth window. This crack had shown signs of opening further, and they feared small fragments falling on the crowded Piazza; so the music was quietly stopped in the hope that the crowd would naturally disperse. The effect was exactly the opposite of that desired. Every one rushed to the Piazza. At eleven I was under the tower which rose in the dim moonlight. The crack was distinctly visible even in this half light, but apparently menaced only a corner of the tower. On Monday early, [the next day] the Campanile was resplendent in the sunshine. At nine...I was near the Rialto sketching. The golden Angel on the tower was shining far away. Suddenly I saw it slowly sink directly downward behind a line of roofs, and a dense grey dust rose in clouds. At once a crowd of people began running across the Rialto towards the Piazza, and I ordered my gondolier to the Piazzetta. On arrival the sight was pitiful. Of that splendid shaft all that remained was a mound of white dust, spreading to the walls of St. Mark's."

Sansovino's marble loggia was promptly restored after the Campanile collapsed in 1902.

In what many Venetians describe as a miracle, no one was injured or killed in the collapse, except for the Campanile custodian's cat. One casualty was the ornate *loggetta*, or loggia, designed by the celebrated Sansovino. Located at the base of the tower, the loggetta was buried under a pile of bricks and rubble over 30 metres (100 feet) high. Amazingly, no other buildings in the piazza were damaged. After the debris was removed, a debate ensued as to whether or not to rebuild the tower. It was quickly decided to rebuild it exactly as it had stood, only this time incorporating a lift.

Why Did It Fall?

Many have speculated about the cause of the Campanile's collapse. Some say workmen removed critical internal supports while others maintain that the dredging of nearby canals caused soil to shift. Others still point to the failure of the 1000-year-old wooden pilings used to shore up the underlying soil. Many consider it a historical question but with many of Venice's other towers leaning so precariously, you can't help but wonder which one will be next.

With donations pouring in from around the world, it took just ten years to rebuild the Campanile and reconstruct Sansovino's loggetta at its base. The Campanile was reopened on St. Mark's Day, 25 April 1912.

Modern Venetian Republicans or Silly Separatists?

Of all the events witnessed by the Master of the House, an event in the last decade ranks near the top of the list for the bizarre and misguided. In the early hours of 9 May 1997, a group of eight men hijacked a vehicle ferry, loaded a makeshift armoured truck and a camper van onto it and ordered the ferry captain to make for the dock at St. Mark's Square. Once there, they disembarked their vehicles, drove onto the square, crashed into the gates and door of the Campanile and made their way to the belfry. Once there, the men unfurled a large banner of the lion of St. Mark and declared themselves to be soldiers of the Most Serene Venetian Government. They did not serve long. The Italian national police arrived with a telescopic ladder that reached to the top of the tower. All of the men surrendered peacefully.

The Rise of the Phoenix

Teatro La Fenice, Campo San Fantin

Venice's premier opera house burns and is rebuilt only to burn and be rebuilt again, like a phoenix.

The mythical phoenix is a large beautiful bird that, at the end of its life, burns itself on a funeral pyre only to be reborn from the ashes and flames, renewed and full of life again. It is with this imagery in mind that you should appreciate Venice's finest and oldest (and ironically newest) opera house—La Fenice, or "The Phoenix" in English. Although Italians from other parts of the country may disagree, Venice is an important opera centre and, along

A golden phoenix stands proudly above La Fenice's sign.

with the Teatro San Carlo in Naples and the Teatro La Scala in Milan, the Teatro La Fenice has been among the elite of Italian opera houses since it opened in the late 18th century.

The Teatro La Fenice traces its beginnings back to an earlier theatre, the San Benedetto. In 1774, the Teatro San Benedetto burned to the ground. Although it was rebuilt, the original owners lost control of the company and struck out to build a new opera house on the Campo San Fantin. Over two dozen plans were submitted for the new building, including Giantonio Selva's winning design. Selva completed the grand structure in just under two years. In 1792, the completed opera house was named La Fenice, as it was a theatre reborn from the flames of its former self. La Fenice opened with a performance of *I Giochi d'Agrigento* by Giovanni Paisiello.

La Fenice was a grand success and its fame spread throughout Italy and Europe, drawing the best composers of the day. But disaster lay just ahead for the theatre. As if holding true to its namesake—the phoenix—the opera house born from the ashes was again reduced to ashes in 1836. This time not a moment was lost and the Meduna brothers, the architects chosen to resurrect the theatre, vowed to rebuild the city treasure exactly as it had been. And they did it within the amazingly short time of one year.

Tinderbox Seats

Being constructed almost entirely out of wood and lit by candles and gas jets, fire was a common occurrence for pre-20th-century theatres in Italy.

The second La Fenice opened the day after Christmas in 1837. In the decades that followed, La Fenice became home to one of the giants of opera, though he was not always showered with success.

Giuseppe Verdi was fairly well known when he first came to Venice and La Fenice to produce *Ernani* in 1844. Venice in the 1840s was under the control of Austria and a tight control is exactly what the northern masters kept the city under, especially its artists. Verdi fought a nearly constant battle to get *Ernani* and later works past the censors and onto the stage. In 1846, he took revenge by writing, despite his poor health, a new work for La Fenice called *Attila*. It was a smashing success due in no small part to the parallels it drew to the Austrian occupation. In the opera, a feared Northern foe threatens a city only to be turned back. *Attila* became a nationalistic work and later served to identify Verdi as an Italian nationalist and pro-unification. In 1851, Verdi brought his revolutionary *Rigoletto* to the stage to rave reviews. The same cannot be said for what would go on to become his most famous work.

Verdi began work on *La Traviata* not long after *Rigoletto*, despite being unwell. His weakened state and a poor cast doomed the première and on 6 March 1853 La Fenice turned on Verdi. Verdi himself describes it best in characterisation of the debut the day after:

"La Traviata was a grand fiasco, and what is worse, they laughed. However, I'm not disturbed about it. Am I wrong, or are they wrong? I believe myself that the last word on La Traviata is not that of last night. They will see it again—and we shall see!"

Thankfully for us, Verdi was a man of supreme confidence and the next year, with a little rework and an improved cast, *La Traviata* opened again, this time at the Teatro San Benedetto, to rave reviews. Despite the setback, Verdi returned to La Fenice and to glory.

The 20th century brought both highs and deep lows for La Fenice. As part of the Biennale artistic celebrations, La Fenice opened many new and important works by such composers as Stravinsky and Prokofiev. By the end of the century, however, La Fenice was showing its age. Therefore, it was closed on 2 January 1996 for repairs that were to take only a few months. With the opera house closed for an electrical upgrade, the city decided to close off the two neighbouring canals for dredging, ironically to allow better access for Venice's fire brigade boats.

As if knowing it was time for a renewal again, a fire broke out in the top rooms of La Fenice on the night of 29 January. With the canals inaccessible, the fire department had no way to respond. The wooden constructed opera house burned all night. In the morning, despondent and despairing Venetians awoke to find La Fenice an empty shell. Foul play was suspected and two electricians working on the project were arrested for arson. They had started the fire in an attempt to cover up the fact that they were behind schedule and, consequently, faced stiff fines from the general contracting company. They faced more than that as they were sentenced to prison in 2001.

Mob Rules?

Conspiracy theories quickly sprung up surrounding the 1996 arson at La Fenice. The electrical contractors were reported to have had connections to organised crime, which might have had the incentive to destroy the landmark in the hope of

Like the mythical bird, La Fenice was consumed and reborn from the flames three times. Nevertheless, it has enjoyed a rich musical heritage throughout all its incarnations. Its sumptuous gilded interior has been host to many prestigious opera premières by artists such as Paisiello, Bellini and Rossini.

lucrative reconstruction contracts. This theory gained considerable currency as the
mob was linked to the arson destruction of the opera house in the southern port
of Bari in 1991.

La Fenice, of course, had to be rebuilt and the first claims of the
city were that the opera house would be reopened in 1998. However,
the building that had been built and rebuilt in two years and one year,
respectively, in previous centuries fell victim to modern Italian red tape
and sloth. By 1998, they had scarcely decided on a contractor to carry
out the repairs and even when they had the company was fired from
the project in 2001. A second company went to work in September
2001. Working 16 hours a day in two shifts (a rarity in Italy), workers
finished the third La Fenice in a respectable time of just over two years
(though it was rumoured that they would not have been able to do so
without the discovery of the Meduna brothers' original plans for the
1837 reconstruction).

The re-rebuilt La Fenice officially opened to the public and gave its
first perform on 12 November 2004. The opening night's performance
was Verdi's *La Traviata*.

The Woman Who Saved Venice

Relief above the Sottoportego del Cappello

An old woman drops a stone vessel from her apartment window and turns the tide in a coup d'etat that threatens the republic. Venice survives the crisis and enjoys nearly five more centuries of republican self-rule.

Following its inception and rise to prominence, Venice was often at odds with Rome (as well as with the rest of Italy). Venice ruled the sea while Rome dominated on land. Venice traded her way to greatness, while Rome ruled through the Church. Venice was a representative republic (a great source of pride for Venetians) while Rome was ruled successively by despotic noble families, as were other parts of Italy. Venice was the city of St. Mark, Rome was the city of St. Peter. Venice had a Doge for a leader while Rome had its pope. These two men of power, who ruled opposing empires, often clashed. In 1309, they clashed over the city of Ferrara located near Venice in northern Italy.

A year earlier, the ruler of Ferrara had died without an heir. In the ensuing power vacuum, two lesser family factions vied for control. One appealed to the Venetian Doge for help, the other to the pope. Venice marched immediately on Ferrara. By the time the pope had been able to send troops from his centre of exile in Avignon, France, he found the city already in Venetian hands. Pope Clement V and his emissaries had no desire to see Ferrara fall into the hands of a growing Venetian empire under Doge Bartolomeo Gradenigo. With its supply lines stretched and facing an army already entrenched in the city, the pope sent an interesting ultimatum to the Doge—retreat from Ferrara or be banned from the Church. The pope did not limit his threat to the Doge. Instead, he extended it to the entire Venetian republic. In addition to the spiritual consequences, excommunication held grave economic and social consequences in the Middle Ages. A person excommunicated from the Church was ineligible to engage in trade and could be sold into slavery. It was an interesting gambit. By threatening the people (and livelihood) of Venice, the pope was taking the issue to the root of the populace. But if the ploy failed, there was always the possibility that it might drive the republic of Venice into the arms of the Byzantine church in Constantinople. Doge Gradenigo held fast, determined to win the standoff. Negotiations and limited hostilities continued throughout the winter. A Venetian delegation made its way to Avignon to find a solution to the crisis but was delayed by spring snows in the Alps. The pope delivered his decree of excommunication for Venice the very day the delegation arrived.

The decree was a disaster for Venice. All members of the clergy were required by the pope to leave the territory of the republic. In all parts of the Mediterranean, Venetian ships and goods were seized. Spurred on by the papal decree against Venice, the cities of Florence, Lucca, Ancona and others joined the forces of the pope and marched on Ferrara. By August 1309, the siege was over and Venice vanquished. With the city of Ferrara lost, the citizens of Venice—now excommunicated and facing financial ruin for nothing—expressed open hostility towards the Doge and his counsel. Most of the dissent came from Venice's older, more conservative and more established families, namely the Querini and Tiepolos. These families felt that Doge Gradenigo had bungled the Ferrara incident from the beginning. Opposing the pope was folly, opposing the pope with arms, as Gradenigo had done, was sacrilege and all of Venice was now paying the price—in this life and in the next. As the demonstrations continued, the Doge's security forces began to crack down. Men began to carry arms in the city and travelled only in groups. Civil war seemed imminent; it only required a spark.

Marco Querini, one of only a handful of survivors from the Ferrara garrison, called together a group of friends and family to formulate a plan to depose Gradenigo. It was to be a three-pronged attack with Marco Querini and Bajamonte Tiepolo attacking from the different sides of the

Doge's Palace while Badoero Badoer crossed the lagoon with his forces and landed next to St. Mark's Square. The date of the attack was set for St. Vitus Day, 15 June 1310. All seemed to be going well with the plot but then the tone of the conspirators seemed to change. Now instead of planning to replace the inept Doge Gradenigo, Bajamonte Tiepolo wished to install himself as supreme leader of Venice and abandon the republic. It is not known if this was the reason why a member of the conspiracy, Marco Donato, defected from the plotters and secretly informed the Doge of the plans.

For all his ineptitude over Ferrara, Gradenigo wasted no time in preparing for the attacks. He summoned troops from the outlying islands and armed the workmen from the Arsenale, all of whom were secretly sequestered inside the Doge's Palace.

A summer storm hit the lagoon on the night of 15 June, stirring up the waters of the lagoon and driving rain into the city. Badoer could not cross the lagoon due to the storm but was not able to warn his counterparts. Unaware, Marco Querini began his advance on St. Mark's Square. His troops shouted "Liberty and death to the Doge" as they marched but their voices could barely be heard above the howling storm. When Querini arrived in the piazza, he found a superior armed force waiting for him. Many of the party, including Marco Querini, were killed in the mêlée and the leaderless group fell back to a nearby campo. Bajamonte Tiepolo, meanwhile, advanced through the rain to the piazza from the opposite direction through a neighbourhood already in uproar, not in support of the coup but in vociferous opposition to the uprising. Tiepolo kept pressing on until the citizens threw more than insults down at him. Just as Tiepolo was entering St. Mark's Square, an old woman tipped a heavy stone mortar out of an upper storey window onto the party below. The stone vessel missed Tiepolo but struck his standard bearer squarely on the head, killing him instantly. Tiepolo, seeing his flag lying in the mud and the open hostility of the Venetians against his plan, broke off the attack and retreated back over the Rialto Bridge to the security of his own neighbourhood. Badoer and his group on the mainland were rounded up, brought to Venice and beheaded.

This stone relief above the entrance into the Sottoportego del Cappello commemorates the events that occurred on the night of 15 June 1310 when the Querini-Tiepolo coup was thwarted by the actions of a loyal supporter of the Venetian republic.

Tiepolo managed to shore up his defences and forced the Doge to offer a settlement of exile from Venice. Tiepolo's house was torn down and a column of infamy (no longer standing) was erected in its place.

The Advent of the Council of Ten

One of the results of the Querini-Tiepolo plot was the introduction of a new governmental body, the Council of Ten. Its purpose was to better check the influence of powerful individuals and the Doge.

When the Doge asked Lucia Rossi, the woman who had tipped the mortar onto Tiepolo's forces at the critical moment of the attempted coup, what the republic could do for her, she replied that she wished only to be allowed to display a banner from her window (no longer standing) on feast days and that her rent never be raised. A white stone tablet inscribed with the date XV-VI-MCCCX (15-6-1310) is set into the street where her stone missile found its mark. A relief of the event is set into the wall above the entrance into the Sottoportego del Cappello.

The date marks the spot—the very place where Lucia Rossi's missile hit Tiepolo's standard bearer.

Viva San Marco

Statue of Daniele Manin, Campo Manin

*Locked in a malaise of foreign rule, one lawyer fights the
system and reestablishes, albeit briefly, the republic of Venice.*

In a secluded campo just off the Rialto stands a statue of one of
Venice's favourite sons, Daniele Manin, a gifted lawyer who turned
his skills to the service of his defeated Venice and nearly freed it.
Manin was born in 1804 into a Venice that was at its ebb. The city
had been in economic decline since the mid-1600s. Napoleon
subsequently arrived in 1797 and ended nearly 1300 years of republican
self-rule and, in the first half of the 19th century, the city was still
under Austrian occupation. Once fiercely proud, the city and its
people no longer had much to be proud about. By the 1840s, Venice
had grown tired of its Austrian overlords. Soldiers and officials
were heckled in the streets while sympathisers of the provisional
government were harassed and their homes vandalised. Venetians
steadfastly refused to applaud any Austrian speech or musical
performances by Austrian military bands in St. Mark's Square. Carnival
was cancelled. Venice was a flammable city, just waiting to go up in
flames.

What's in a Name?

Daniele Manin had a famous name but it was not his own. Daniele's father was a
converted Jew who took the name of the man who converted him to Christianity,
Pietro Manin. Pietro Manin was the brother of Lodovico Manin, the last Doge of
Venice.

Manin studied law at the nearby University of Padua and then
moved back to Venice, where he gained a reputation in the city as a

good litigator. Like many young men of his time, Manin was interested in the nationalist and Italian unification movements of the time but there was little he could about it living in a city under direct military rule. Except where the law was concerned.

In January 1848, Manin drafted a petition to the Austrian emperor in which he detailed the grievances of the Venetian people and the numerous ways the provisional military government had violated previous promises made to the city. It did not take the Austrians long to respond.

Daniele Manin was arrested on 18 January and taken to the notorious Leads prison in the Doge's Palace. But Manin had already become an advocate for the people and his arrest only served to stir up further unrest. After two months of increasingly intense protest, angry rioters surrounded the Doge's Palace, where the Austrian governor resided, and demanded that Manin be released. When the crowd began hammering at the palace doors, the governor consented. With their advocate free, the city fell into riotous celebration. The following days were more like chaos. The governor, fearing a full insurrection should he use force to reinstall order, appealed to Manin for calm. Manin agreed to do what he could if he could form a civil guard to assist him. It was agreed and a 2000-man force was at Manin's disposal in less than a day. Manin and force restored some semblance of order to the city, but it was to be short-lived.

On 22 March, a mob of Arsenale workers brutally murdered the Austrian appointed commander of the Arsenale, Venice's longtime shipyard, naval port and armoury. Daniele Manin left his office and set out alone for the Arsenale to investigate. But word spread quickly and, by the time he arrived, Manin was surrounded by 100 members of the new Civil Guard. Manin and the Civil Guard arrived just before the Austrian reinforcements and he seized the opportunity. He ordered the Arsenale to be opened and the contents of the armoury distributed to the Civil Guard and the Italian workers of the Arsenale. The Civil Guard was now an army and Austrian rule hung by a thread. Manin rallied the Guard round him and delivered a passionate speech in which he proclaimed a new Venetian republic. He ended the speech with the famous "Viva San Marco", a phrase that had not been used openly in Venice for half a century.

Venice was a republic once more; its pride regained and its citizens armed. The Austrians recognised their position to be untenable and abandoned the city to Manin and his forces. They were not gone for long.

Manin quickly set up a new government in Venice with himself as president. The new republic instituted new legislative bodies, courts and even printed its own money but the honeymoon was short-lived. Twelve months later, the Austrians returned and they intended to regain the city.

First Aerial Bombardment

Venice has the distinction of being the first city to be bombarded from the air as Austrian forces devised a clever, though poorly executed, plan to drop bombs from a fleet of hot air balloons.

The Austrian forces laid siege to Venice from both the land and the sea. Hope was fading in the city and Manin broached the subject of surrender. The Venetian Assembly, however, voted to resist at all costs, and cost it would. The bread ran out first, spreading panic through the city as prices soared and women in the markets were seen tearing the earrings from their ears and wedding rings from their fingers to pay for the precious loaves. Citizens then turned to fish but the appetites of Venice's 200,000 inhabitants soon exhausted the lagoon's supply (not to mention that fishermen had to ply their nets under enemy fire). Artillery bombardment followed shortly after as the Austrians brought their guns to elevated positions at the edge of the mainland in order to reach the city. Just one or two projectiles fell at first but eventually numbered around 40 an hour, 24 hours a day, rendering a deep psychological effect on the city. Disease was the final blow to an already desperate city. A cholera epidemic broke out in July 1849, killing several thousand. It was clear to everyone that the end was at hand for the reborn republic.

Venetian envoys boarded gondolas headed for the mainland flying white flags. In the conditions for peace, the Austrians stated that the city would be spared if the Austrians were welcomed back into the city and if Manin and the others responsible for the revolt were exiled. Considering the circumstances, these seemed liberal terms indeed and Manin and 40 others boarded a ship for France as the Austrians returned. Manin, having spent his entire fortune in the defence of Venice, lived in Paris and taught Italian until his death in 1857. His statue in Campo Manin was erected in 1875 by the government of a free Italy.

Manin Looks Away

The status of Daniele Manin in Campo Manin looks in the direction of where his home once stood. The campo also hosts one of Venice's few new buildings, the uninspired Cassa di Risparmio Bank. Local legend is quickly forgetting what the bronze Manin was originally looking at, saying instead that the statue is averting its eyes from the hideous façade of the bank.

145

You Build It, You Break It, You Buy It

Library of St. Mark's, Piazzetta San Marco

Venice commissions its favourite architect to construct a grand building on St. Mark's Square but when a portion of the project collapses, the punishment for the builder is swift and harsh.

Venice has long been a refuge for those fleeing oppression, war and tyranny. It was three such refugees whose combined gifts contributed to the creation of one of the greatest libraries in the world.

Petrarch is considered to be one of the fathers of the Renaissance. Born in Tuscany near Florence, his family had to flee Florence when he was an infant. He lived in France, Spain, Germany, Rome and, eventually, Venice. He reportedly liked Venice so much that he donated his entire collection of ancient manuscripts to the city in exchange for the use of a house in the *sestiere* of Castello. The city received these works and housed them in the Doge's Palace as a temporary measure.

Nearly 100 years later in 1453, the Ottoman Turks captured the city of Constantinople, ending its nearly 1500 unbroken years as the capital of Western civilisation. With the fall of Constantinople, a flood of refugees flocked to Venice's shores. One of these refugees was Cardinal Bessarion, the patriarch of Constantinople and one of the most learned and scholarly men of his time. Like Petrarch, Bessarion spent the better part of his life collecting and interpreting ancient Latin and Greek texts. His collection of over a thousand classical texts was priceless. In choosing a place to take his collection (and himself), Venice's stability and resemblance to that of an ancient Greek republican government weighed heavily. He moved to Venice and donated his entire collection to the city.

The only question now was where to house Bessarion's and Petrarch's priceless and extensive collections. It would be another 80 years before a structure would be laid out to house the collections permanently and, once again, a refugee would come to Venice's service.

Jacopo Sansovino, like many in Renaissance Italy, was a man of multiple and extreme talents. Born in Florentine, he was a contemporary of Michelangelo, to whom his sculptures were favourably compared. Sansovino completed many works for clients in Florence and Rome but he left his mark in the field of architecture—particularly in Venice, his new home after fleeing Rome following its sacking by enraged Lutherans in 1527.

Sansovino brought a new appreciation for architecture to Venice, a city whose landmark buildings and main square had fallen into disrepair. His first contract for the city was to revamp St. Mark's Square, which was overrun with small food stalls, makeshift hostels and other rabble. Next, the Senate contracted him to shore up the sagging and tired domes of St. Mark's Basilica. Sansovino remedied the old wooden domes by adding internal supports and encircling the domes with taut iron chains. The Senate was so pleased with his solution that they offered him the position of *protomaestro*, a combination of state architect and superintendent of buildings. It was a very prestigious appointment and provided him with many contracts in the city, including a few palazzos along the Grand Canal. However, three of his finest works are to be seen in St. Mark's Square and the adjoining Piazzetta San Marco, namely the lovely *loggetta*, or loggia, at the base of the towering Campanile; the *Zecca*, or Mint; and the Library of St. Mark's, which stands opposite the Doge's Palace.

An Interesting Fundraiser

Located right behind the Library of St. Mark's, Sansovino's *Zecca*, or Mint, of Venice was financed with a unique tax. Under a law introduced by the Senate, slaves under

Venetian control on the island of Cyprus were allowed their freedom for a price of 50 ducats. Within two years, the entire project was paid for.

Sansovino was awarded the commission for the library to house Petrarch's and Bessarion's collections in 1537. He fully understood the importance of the commission as well as fully appreciated the prime nature of the location in St. Mark's Square. He set about designing a neoclassical masterpiece, a library to rival the one lost in Alexandria.

The ornate façade of St. Mark's Library. The library today houses the national library of St. Mark's, the Biblioteca Nazionale Marciana.

Construction began the following year. The building was going well until December 1545 when a large half-constructed vault collapsed without warning. Sansovino blamed the failure on a heavy winter frost, on vibrations caused by cannons and on workers who had removed critical supports. The Senate was not interested in excuses and was not used to a state architect failing at his job. Sansovino was quickly imprisoned on grounds of incompetence. His salary was also suspended. Sansovino sat in prison until several of his colleagues, Titian among them, lobbied the Senate for his release. The Senate agreed to release him on the condition that he paid for the repair work out of his own pocket. Sansovino agreed and set about repairing the damage.

It took him 20 years to pay back the entire cost of the repair work. Thankfully, the incident was largely forgotten by then and he had a host of contracts from which to choose. The library was finished in 1591, almost 20 years after Sansovino's death.

INSIDER'S TIPS

St. Mark's Basilica One of the true treasures of the world, the piazza and the basilica have been wowing visitors for hundreds of years now. If visiting the basilica in the high season (summer especially), get there early as the queues can be long. Free but there are small fees to visit attractions inside the basilica (all are worth it). Open 9.45am–4.45pm (October to March); 9.45am–5pm (April to September). St. Mark's Square. Website: www.basilicasanmarco.it/

Doge's Palace The home to the leaders of Venice for 600 years, this building is the ultimate palazzo. The Doge's Palace is home to countless artworks (there are English-language explanations in each room) and is on the must-see list. Euro 11, reduced to Euro 5.50 with VENICECard. Open 9am–5pm (November to March); 9am–7pm (April to October). Ticket office closes one hour before closing time. Piazzetta San Marco. Tel: 041 2715911. Website: www.museiciviciveneziani. it/main.asp?lin=EN

Of interest is the Secret Itineraries tour of the Doge's Palace (available three times a morning in English). This ninety-minute tour goes behind the scenes at the Doge's Palace to cover the history and use of some of the bureaucratic offices, torture chambers and the notorious Leads prison where Casanova was held. Reservations required and can be difficult to get in the summer. Euro 12.50 (includes admission to the rest of the Doge's Palace) or Euro 7 with VENICECard. English-language tours start at 9.55am, 10.45am and 11.35am. Tel: 041 5207090.

Museo Correr Did you ever wonder what's in the buildings surrounding St. Mark's Square? It's this museum. It's quite nice with exhibits portraying the history of Venice, classical sculpture and Renaissance painting. Euro 11, reduced to Euro 5.50 with VENICECard. Open 9am–5pm (November to March); 9am–6pm (April to October). Ticket office closes one hour before closing time. St. Mark's Square. Tel: 041 2405211. Website: www.museiciviciveneziani.it/main. asp?lin=EN

Library of St. Mark's This is one of the best libraries in the country. Entry is included with the entrance fee to the Museo Correr. Artworks include ones by Tintoretto, Titian and Veronese. Open 8.10am–7pm Monday to Friday, 8.10am–1.30pm Saturday. Piazzetta San Marco. Tel: 041 2407211. Website: http://marciana.venezia.sbn.it/ (Italian only)

Campanile Want an unbelievable view of the city? Get it at the top of the tallest tower in Venice. Try not to be in the belfry on the hour as the bells are deafening. Euro 6. Open 9.45am–4pm (October to March); 9.30am–5pm (April to June); 9.45am–8pm (July to September). St. Mark's Square. Website: www.basilicasanmarco.it/

Church of San Moise From the exterior, this does not appear to be one of Venice's more beautiful churches but it does house artworks by Tintoretto and Palma the Younger. Noted courtesan Veronica Franco is reputed to be buried somewhere in the church. Free. Open 3.30pm–5pm Monday to Saturday, 9am–noon Sunday. Campo San Moise.

Church of Santa Maria del Giglio This Palladian-style church houses works by Palma the Younger and Tintoretto, as well as a rare (in Venice) painting attributed to Rubens. Euro 2.50 or Chorus Pass. Open 10am–5pm Monday to Saturday, 1pm–5pm Sunday. Campo Santa Maria del Giglio.

Church of San Salvador This surprisingly large church is lost in the throngs of commerce going on outside. Pop in for a respite from the crush of people outside and for a look at the two Titian paintings inside. The floor is amazing. Free. Open 9am–noon, 3pm–6pm Monday to Saturday, 3pm–6pm Sunday; 9am–noon, 4pm–6pm Monday to Saturday, 4pm–6pm Sunday June to August. Merceria San Salvador. Tel: 041 5236717. Website: www.chiesasansalvador.it/en/home_e.html

Hotel Panada Good value for money, this three-star hotel is just two streets away from St. Mark's Square. Singles between Euro 119–259, Doubles between Euro 145–310. Calle Specchieri. Tel: 041 5209088. Website: www.hotelpanada.com

Hotel Saturnia This is my favourite hotel in the city. The lobby and interior of this four-star hotel are furnished in classic Venetian style while the rooms are modern with all the comforts. The staff is wonderful. Singles from Euro 112–280, doubles from Euro 180–450, triples from Euro 369–615. Calle Larga 22 Marzo. Tel: 041 5208377. Website: www. venice-hotel.hotelsaturnia.it/

Hotel Concordia Billed as the only hotel with a view of St. Mark's Square, this four-star hotel is also within earshot of the bells of the Campanile (not for the light sleeper). Singles between Euro 120–240, doubles between Euro 180–400. 367 Calle Larga San Marco. Tel: 041 5206866. Website: www.hotelconcordia.com

Hotel Centauro Tucked away from the bustle of it all is the three-star Centauro. Singles from Euro 28 without bath and from Euro 50 with bath. Doubles from Euro 55 without bath to Euro 110 for a double with a canal view. 4297/A Calle della Vida. Tel: 041 5225832. Website: www.hotelcentauro.com

Casa Arte Located near Campo San Stefano, this small three-star hotel is a short walk from many of the city's major attractions. Calle del Frutariol. Tel: 041 5200882. Website: www.casaarte.info

Caffé Florian This café has been serving coffee in St. Mark's Square since 1720. Pop in to find out why. This place is a landmark more than any other café or eatery in Venice. St. Mark's Square. Tel: 041 5205641. Website: www.caffeflorian.com

Osteria Enoteca San Marco This is what a good restaurant should be—a wine list like a phone book and a menu on a single page. Delicious, but usually full (get there early or call ahead). Euro 15–25 per plate. Frezzeria. Tel: 041 5285242.

Trattoria Do Forni Self proclaimed as "the restaurant in Venice", it is certainly among the best. Great service. Euro 15–25 per plate. Calle degli Specchieri. Tel: 041 5238880. Website: www.doforni.it/eng/frame_ristorante.htm

Osteria Ai Assassini Literally "The Killer's Restaurant", this osteria puts its tongue firmly in its cheek as it plays on the name of this once dangerous street in Venice. The neighbourhood is better now and so is the food now that this place is open. Great wine list, too. Calle d. Assassini. Tel: 041 5287986. Website: www.osteriaaiassassini.it

Chet qui rit Looking for a quick no-fuss fill up for you or the family? This is the place to go near St. Mark's Square. This self-service buffet is quick, cheap and easy (rarely found in Venice). Closed Saturday. Frezzeria. Tel: 041 5229086.

Harry's Bar A Venetian landmark since World War II and a well-worn watering hole. Quite expensive. Calle Vallaresso. Tel: 041 5285777. Website: www.cipriani.com

Linda Gonzales Shops off the beaten track include this lovely little hand-bound book and mask shop near La Fenice. Campo San Fantin.

Mille Vini Did you find a great wine at one of the recommended enotecas and want to get a bottle (or a case) to take home? Check out Mille Vini (or "1000 Wines" in English). Via Fapanni.

Vivaldi Store Can't get enough Vivaldi? Fill up here with CDs, books, calendars, sheet music and more. Campo San Bartolomeo. Tel: 041 5221343.

Petra Prints, statues and antiques of Venice distributed between two nearby stores. This might be the perfect place to find that gift for the person who has everything. Calle Larga 22 Marzo. Tel: 041 5231815.

Fiorella Gallery Get your custom-made jacket from artist Fiorella Mancini. Of particular interest are the hand-carved wooden female mannequins with high heels and heads of Venetian doges. Campo San Stefano. Tel: 063203500. Website: www.fiorellagallery.com

Rigattieri This is the only store in Venice where I could find Capo di Monte ceramics. The owner is friendly and loves to talk about Capo di Monte. Between Campo Sant'Angelo and Campo San Stefano. Tel: 041 5231081. Website: www.rigattieri-venice.com/

NetHouse One of the few internet cafés in Venice. Campo San Stefano. Tel: 041 5224657. Website: www.nethousecafes.com

It seems like all of San Marco is a shop. Gucci, Prada, Spiga, Magli, Bvlgari, and more, are all in this neighbourhood. A shopper's paradise. There are two main routes to follow for exclusive shopping: St. Mark's Square to the Rialto following the Merceria onto Rio S. Zulian and then towards the Rialto. Or St. Mark's Square towards Campo San Moise and Campo Santa Maria del Giglio.

Short Walk

Starting Point—St. Mark's Square. Head to the closed end of the piazza and walk along Salizz. San Moise until you reach Campo S. Moise. From here, cross the canal and follow the Calle Larga 22 Marzo. Cross the Rio dell'Albergo into Campo Santa Maria Zobenigo. Cross the canal and follow the Calle Zaguri into Campo San Maurizio. Exit along C. le Spezier, cross the canal and you will find yourself in the Campo San Stefano, one of Venice's liveliest squares. Walk past the Church of San Stefano and follow the Calle le Frati into the Campo Sant'Angelo. From there, take the Calle Spezier, the Calle Mandola and the Calle Cortesia, respectively, over to the Campo Manin, which contains the statue of the 19th-century lawyer turned revolutionary Daniele Manin. Take the exit at the back left-hand side of the campo, Calle Cavalli, and follow it all the way to the Grand Canal. Turn right onto Riva del Carbon and follow it until you reach the Rialto Bridge.

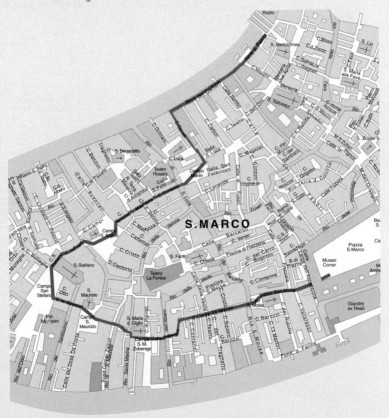

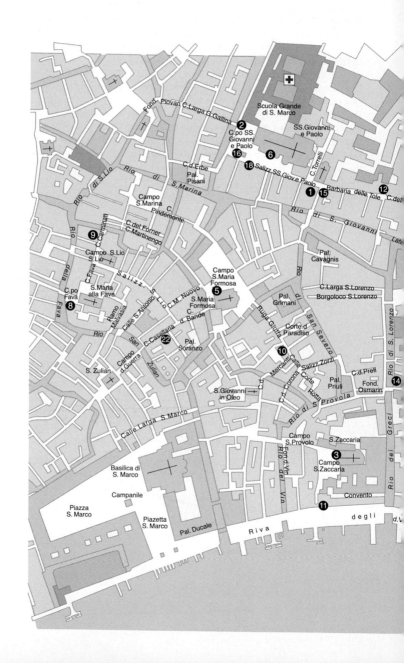

Key for Castello

1. Birreria alla Strega
2. Campo dei Santi Giovanni e Paolo
3. Church of San Zaccaria
4. Church of Santa Maria della Visitazione (La Pietà)
5. Church of Santa Maria Formosa
6. Church of Santi Giovanni e Paolo
7. Corte Sconta
8. Flavia
9. Giovanna Zanella
10. Hotel Al Piave
11. Hotel Paganelli
12. Internet Corner
13. La Residenza
14. Liassidi Palace
15. Locanda Giovanni e Paolo
16. Monument to Colleoni
17. Museo Storico Navale (Naval History Museum)
18. Rosa Salva
19. Scuola of San Giorgio delgi Schiavoni
20. Torri dell'Arsenale (Arsenale Gates)
21. Trattoria Al Scalinetto
22. Venetian Navigator

Bragadin's Skin

Bragadin's Urn, Church of Santi Giovanni e Paolo,
Campo dei Santi Giovanni e Paolo

A Venetian captain is betrayed and brutally martyred in defence of the republic but part of him is brought back to a final resting place.

Throughout much of the late medieval and into the Renaissance period, the Venetian republic was an empire on the march both on land and at sea. With many lucrative trading routes and distant ports of call to protect, Venice expanded its interests behind the points of swords and under the sails of its warships. In time, it ruled over lands beyond the modern Italian state of Veneto, much of the Dalmatian coast (modern-day Croatia) and remote outposts such as Corfu

The Church of Santi Giovanni e Paolo—where Captain Bragadin was finally laid to rest.

and Crete. By the second half of the 16th century, the Ottoman Turks had begun to threaten Venetian interests in the eastern Mediterranean, specifically Venetian-controlled Cyprus.

By 1570, Venice had controlled the island of Cyprus for just over 80 years, using a governor, who reported back to the Venetian Senate, to control a largely feudally based society. The Cypriots had no love for this remote governance, which proved disastrous to both themselves and their Venetian lords when the Turks came calling.

On 3 July 1570, the Turks landed 350 warships in a remote coastal area of Cyprus under the banner of Ottoman Sultan Selim II. Cyprus was doomed from the moment these ships were anchored. The island lay nearly 1500 nautical miles away from Venice and its Arsenale while it lay less than 160 kilometres from Turkish soil (and Turkish reinforcements). By the time the Turks were assembled at the gates of Nicosia and later at Famagusta, they had a well-equipped force of 200,000 against a besieged force of one-tenth that number. Good leadership might have narrowed the manpower gap but here, too, Venice came up short. The Cypriot governor, Nicolo Dandolo, was most likely a severe manic-depressive. His wild swings from a flurry of often nonsensical activities to base catatonia led many on the island to believe that he was in the employ of the sultan. What's worse, he was charged with the defence of Nicosia, the Turks' first target.

The Turkish forces arrived at Nicosia and proceeded to lay siege to the city. The Turkish commander offered terms of surrender to the city—surrender the island now in the face of overwhelming numbers and keep the favour of the sultan or face his wrath. Dandolo, inert in depression, did nothing. The Turks made good on their word. The ensuing 45-day siege of Nicosia did little more than reduce the Venetian ranks and anger the Turkish commanders, who subsequently allowed their forces to freely plunder the city in a seven-day orgy of rape, pillage and destruction. Dandolo and his ever-shrinking forces retreated to the governor's palace on the main city square. On the final day of fighting in the city, Dandolo, no doubt manic, donned his most stately gubernatorial vestments, exited the palace (with his forces still fighting around him) and descended the steps into the square to be received and given the preferential treatment due to an official of his rank. A Turkish officer, sword drawn, quickly approached and decapitated him.

On the other end of the island, the military garrison town of Famagusta—and Venice's last hope for Cyprus—prepared for the worst under the skilled leadership of Marcantonio Bragadin. The defensive walls were refortified, battlements reinforced and the 7000-strong force was drilled in preparation for the arrival of the sultan's 200,000 soldiers. Two days after the fall of Nicosia, the Turks arrived at Famagusta to present Bragadin with terms of surrender and Dandolo's head. Bragadin rejected the terms and the siege of Famagusta began. Unlike Dandolo's disaster at Nicosia, Bragadin fought masterfully, drawing out the siege for 11 months. When his forces had dwindled from 7000 to less than 700 and when this meagre force had eaten everything in the town, including their own cavalry horses, Captain Bragadin sent emissaries to discuss terms of surrender with the Turks. The military convention of the day prescribed that a city conquered after a siege was subject to plunder, but a city that surrendered after a siege would be spared these indignities and its defenders would garner respectful treatment. The returning Turkish terms were generous: Bragadin and his men could embark from Famagusta and enjoy an unmolested journey to Venetian-controlled Crete. The terms came with a letter from the Turkish commanders complimenting Bragadin on his skilful defence of the town.

The first few days preparing for the departure went well. Provisions were brought into the town, the sick and dying were treated and ships were prepared for departure. All was going well until Bragadin and his staff met with the Turkish commander Mustafa to deliver the keys to the town. At first, Mustafa received his guests with respect but, during the course of the procession, he became angry and eventually violent. He drew a knife and cut off Bragadin's right ear, then ordered an aid to cut off the other one. Most of the Venetian captain's staff was killed on the spot, with a few escaping. In the following hours, the Turks killed as many Venetians as they could find. Reportedly, 350 disembodied heads were piled up in front of the Turkish command.

Captain Bragadin survived the day and was thrown into prison for two weeks where his wounds festered. The Turks then dragged him around the city and tied him to a chair atop the yardarm of a ship to be taunted by the troops. From there, they took him to the town square, tied him to a column and flayed the skin from his body. Legend states that Bragadin remained silent throughout the ordeal and expired when the torturers reached his waist. His skin was then stuffed with straw and paraded around the town tied to the back of a cow. The Turks took Bragadin's skin back to Constantinople and presented it as a trophy to the sultan. Nine years later however, a Venetian named Girolamo Polidoro, one of the few escapees from the Turkish treachery at Famagusta, somehow stole the skin from Constantinople and returned it to Venice, where it was installed in a funerary niche high in the walls of the Church of Santi Giovanni e Paolo, also known as San Zanipolo. It remains there today.

Bragadin's funerary niche in the Church of Santi Giovanni e Paolo. When the niche was opened for inspection during restoration works in 1961, it was found to contain a small lead casket with several pieces of tanned human skin inside.

Battle of Lepanto

The loss of Cyprus and the memory of the horrific death of Marcantonio Bragadin at the hands of the Turks was short-lived. Later that year, the Venetians, in alliance with Pope Pius V and King Philip II of Spain, dealt the Ottoman Empire a blow by defeating them soundly at the famous naval battle of Lepanto.

The Arsenale

Torri dell'Arsenale (Arsenale Gates), Campo Arsenale

A burgeoning sea power consolidates shipbuilding into a state-sponsored industry and rises to rule the waves.

With its absence of roads and automobiles, its abundance of watercraft of all types and buildings that seem built directly on the water, Venice appears, as Lord Byron said, to have risen directly from the sea. One thing is for sure—regardless of whether or not Venice was born from the sea, all Venetians were. Venetians have always done everything on the water; it is where they are most comfortable, which is why when the young republic ventured forth to stake its claim in the world it did so under the shadow of sails and the strain of oars. But seafarers are only as good as their ships and when you mention ships and shipbuilding to the Venetians, they will swell with pride and tell you about the Arsenale.

Origin of the Word

We think of the word "arsenal" as having always been part of the English lexicon but it was contributed by the Venetians. The word derives from the Arabic *Dar Sina'a,* or "house of industry". The word was incorporated into the English language via Dante, who described the boiling pitch pots of the Arsenale in his descriptions of hell.

At the turn of the first millennium, Venice was already an established shipbuilding state. It had many small *squeri*, or shipyards, dotted throughout the lagoon. But under the visionary leadership of Doge Ordelafo Falier in the early 12th century, Venice consolidated its large shipbuilding enterprises into a natural lagoon at the east end of the

Castello district. Over the following decades, a vast complex of docks, foundries, shops, homes for workers and fortifications sprang up around this lagoon. Soon, the area came to have its own name, the Arsenale. One of the first developments in the Arsenale was the advent of assembly line production. Ship styles and sizes were standardised and labour was divided among smaller teams working on individual components such as keels, spars, prows and masts, which could then be assembled as part of a standard process. This process also meant that manufactured ships could be more easily maintained.

The Hunger for Raw Materials

The rate at which ships were produced in the Arsenale was legendary, but so too was its insatiable thirst for raw materials, namely timber, to construct those ships. Most of the trees used to construct the ships came across the Adriatic from the Dalmatian coast of present-day Croatia.

This mass production of both merchant ships and warships elevated Venice's position in the Mediterranean, an elevation that soon brought more profits to the city. In 1200, the Christian powers of Europe embarked on a fresh Crusade to again retake the Holy Land from the infidels. The next year, a delegation of French knights arrived in Venice to procure transport vessels to Palestine. The Doge was more than happy to accommodate them, for a fee of course (half of the expedition's plunder). With the price fixed, the workers of the Arsenale, the *Arsenalotti*, floated the ships very quickly so that the Crusaders could transport their 4500 knights and horses and 30,000 foot soldiers to the Middle East.

The Size of a Town

The Arsenalotti, or the workers of the Arsenale, numbered 16,000 at their peak in the 16th century, the equivalent to the population of a city in Renaissance Italy.

In the early 14th century, Dante travelled to Venice and visited the Arsenale to see the unique way in which the Arsenalotti assembled the ships. He went on to describe this assembly line production in his *Inferno*:

"As in the Arsenal of the Venetians, in winter, the sticky pitch for smearing their unsound vessels is boiling, because they cannot go to sea, and, instead therefore, one builds him a new bark, and one caulks the sides of that which hath made many a voyage; one hammers at the prow, and one at the stern; another makes oars, and another twists ropes; another patches the jib and mainsail."

The gates leading into the Arsenale. The Arsenale is now an Italian naval base and is off limits to the public. However, you can access a part of it, the Arsenale Vecchio (the original Arsenale), by taking Vaporetto 41, 42 or 5.

It was about the time of Dante's visit that the Arsenale underwent its first expansion. With a new addition, the *Arsenale Nuove* (New Arsenale), the complex was expanded to four times its original size. The new Arsenale focused almost entirely on new vessel construction while the final outfitting was done in the original section. In the early 16th century, the shipyard was expanded once again, this time to house a large-scale dry dock and to store constructed ships ready for use in a state emergency. This came in handy in 1570.

By the middle of the 16th century, Venice had a new rival on the waves, the Ottoman Turks. In 1570, the Turks invaded Venetian-controlled Cyprus and laid siege to the cities of Nicosia and Famagusta. Venice put everything that would float into the sea to provide relief for the doomed defenders and the Arsenalotti constructed, completely outfitted and floated an astonishing 100 war galleys in just two months. These galleys proved vital at the Battle of Lepanto.

But perhaps the most famous demonstration of Venice's maritime prowess and shipbuilding efficiency was given to King Henri III of France. He visited the Arsenale and saw the workers putting together the backbone of a hull. He then returned to the Doge's Palace to enjoy a state banquet. By the time the banquet had ended, the backbone of the hull that he had seen earlier was now a completed ship floating in the Grand Canal before the palace.

Models of Success

It was common in pre-industrial Italy for shipwrights to work from scale models instead of from drawings or blueprints. Many of the models seen in the Museo Storico Navale (Naval History Museum) were rescued from the Arsenale by workers just before Napoleon's destruction of the yards.

The Arsenale continued to produce ships, though at a much-reduced capacity, up until the end of the republic. Goethe visited the yard in 1786 and said of the remaining workers that it was "like visiting some old family which, though past its prime, still showed signs of life." Napoleon's invasion in 1797 put an end to that when he sacked the Arsenale and took the remaining ships in an attempt to invade Ireland. The Austrians then used it to build a number of warships during World War I but it has remained mostly idle since then. Today, the Arsenale is under the administration of the Italian Navy although there are rumours that it may be converted to public use.

The Church of the Red Priest

Church of Santa Maria della Visitazione (Church of La Pietà),
Riva degli Schiavoni

*A sickly priest with a musical gift rises from obscurity to the
heights of fame and society, only to lose it all.*

Situated on the Riva degli Schiavoni waterfront promenade just east of the Doge's Palace and St. Mark's Square sits a small church with a giant musical legacy. The full name of the church is Santa Maria della Visitazione but Venetians simply call it La Pietà. The current church was rebuilt in 1746 on the site of an earlier church dating back to the 1400s. However, La Pietà's roots run even deeper than that; the institution for which La Pietà eventually became famous dates back to the mid-1300s. The current church of La Pietà was once one of four refuges-cum-convents that catered exclusively to abandoned or orphaned girls in the city. Any infant girl born out of marriage, abandoned by poor or abusive parents or orphaned by the death of her parents could find comfort and care within the walls of La Pietà until she became an adult. There was only one catch— she had to study, perfect and perform music. The reason being that La Pietà and the other three convents were among some of the finest music schools in Italy, in which the girls practised diligently and performed regularly scheduled public concerts. The proceeds of the concerts went towards supporting the convent and the school and towards the dowries for girls who might wish to marry when they became old enough. In the early 18th century, La Pietà became more famous than its three sister schools thanks to the efforts of its music teacher, a priest and violinist who went on to become a giant of classical music.

Antonio Vivaldi was born in Venice on 4 March 1678, the son of a professional violinist who played at the city's finest venues, including St. Mark's. As a baby, Vivaldi was so sickly that his nanny secretly took the newborn to be baptised for fear he might die. He did little to outgrow the condition and was plagued all his life by what he called *strettezza di petto* (tightness of the chest), which was most likely asthma. From an early age, Vivaldi's parents had decided that their son was to enter the priesthood. He entered at age 15 and was ordained a priest ten years later. Despite his commitment to the order, Vivaldi continued to master the violin, often practising with his father and sometimes filling in for him at concerts. Vivaldi continued to suffer badly from asthma and was exempted from performing (speaking) Mass because he could never complete it without gasping for breath and nearly collapsing. In time, it became much easier for Vivaldi to express himself through music. Leading, in essence, a double life of mute priest and burgeoning maestro, the future seemed uncertain for Vivaldi until a very unique opportunity presented itself.

The Red Priest

Antonio Vivaldi, like his father, had a full head of bright red hair, which was quite uncommon in Italy. His violinist father had been nicknamed *Rossi*, meaning "red". When Vivaldi became an ordained priest in 1703, he gained the nickname *Il Prete Rosso*, or "the Red Priest". The name stuck, even after Vivaldi had made his name in the music world.

At the end of 1703, Vivaldi was offered the position of violin teacher at La Pietà. Since the position was at a church-run orphanage, he was required to remain within his priestly vestments. He instructed the girls in violin but had enough free time to begin composing stringed and vocal works. His first work, a collection of violin sonatas, was published and first performed in Venice in 1705. Vivaldi continued to teach at La Pietà and to compose. In 1712, he published and performed his second opus, the famous *L'estro armonico*, for solo violin. This work was also successfully published in Amsterdam and circulated throughout much of northern and central Europe. Over the next few years, and under the direction of Maestro Vivaldi, La Pietà gained a reputation for its concerts that grew beyond the lagoon and even beyond the Veneto. Soon, any visit to the city was incomplete without attending a concert at La Pietà.

Lying to Get In

The reputation of La Pietà grew to such stature and the education granted to the girls was so superior to what was available elsewhere in the city that parents tried to pass off their infant daughters as orphans so that they could go to the prestigious school. The situation became so blatant that a warning plaque was set into the outer wall of the church threatening excommunication to those who attempted to leave their children to the school without need. The plaque is still there today.

By 1718, Vivaldi's reputation had grown so much that the school of La Pietà could no longer hold him. He travelled and composed in Mantua and Vicenza, experimenting with opera for the first time.

Antonio Vivaldi wrote many pieces of music while he taught at La Pietà. In total, he is accredited with roughly 500 concertos. More than 300 are for solo instruments, of these about 230 are written for the violin.

In 1723, Vivaldi returned to Venice and to La Pietà. However, he only composed and staged performances as his frequent travels made teaching effectively impossible. It was back in Venice and at La Pietà that Vivaldi met the love of his life.

Anna Giraud was a young contralto from La Pietà. Vivaldi claimed she possessed a classical voice, though others disagreed. She soon began to accompany the maestro on his trips and her sister Paolina also accompanied them, ostensibly as Vivaldi's nurse. Scandal quickly followed as rumours flew that both his protégé,

Anna, and his nurse attended to all the maestro's physical needs, even the carnal ones. It was even rumoured that Vivaldi and Anna were secretly married.

From 1729 to 1739, Vivaldi, Anna and Paolina travelled extensively, stopping at numerous cities in Germany, Amsterdam, Prague, Rome, Verona and finally Ferrara, where the papal nuncio, Cardinal Ruffo, refused Vivaldi entry into the city to stage his latest opera because he was a priest who did not say Mass and who lived with two unmarried women. Vivaldi, shaken by the disciplinary action in Ferrara, returned to Venice to sell his vocal and instrumental compositions to La Pietà. He wrote operas in Venice but his popularity had declined by then as the public had been captivated by the whimsical *commedia del'arte*, or comedy of masks, works of Goldoni.

Vivaldi travelled to Vienna at the invitation of Austrian Emperor Charles VI in 1740 but his patron, the emperor, died shortly after his arrival and Vienna quickly fell into political chaos. It was hardly a conducive environment in which to make a living as a musician or a nearly defrocked Catholic priest. Vivaldi fell ill and died in relative anonymity in Vienna the following year. He was buried in a simple, state-sponsored ceremony with his Requiem Mass sung by six choirboys, one of whom was a young Joseph Haydn.

La Pietà, now as it was in Vivaldi's day, is more of a concert venue than a church and it regularly hosts recitals of its old maestro's works.

Taking Your Time

The reconstruction of La Pietà was begun in 1746 by Giorgio Massari but was not completed until 1906, taking a total of 160 years.

Wed to the Sea

Bucintoro model, Museo Storico Navale (Naval History Museum),
Campo San Biagio

*In a centuries-old ceremony beloved by Venetians, their leader sails every
year in his royal galley to the Lido to marry the Adriatic Sea.*

In a corner of Room 16 in the
Museo Storico Navale near the
Arsenale sits a scaled wooden
model of one of the most unique
ships to ever take to water, the
famous *Bucintoro*, the Doge's
personal galley. The size of a
full ocean-going ship, it was, in
various forms, the state vessel of
Venice from 1277 to 1798. The
Bucintoro was always at the ready
for the Doge although he often
put it at the disposal of visiting
dignitaries such as King Henri III
of France who arrived in Venice
from the mainland in the royal

*The elaborate gilded bow of the Doge's
Bucintoro.*

ship. However, the most famous use for the *Bucintoro* was its annual trip
sailing the Doge from his palace to a small church on the Lido where,
in a state ceremony, he would marry the sea.

The Doge's Marriage to the Sea is a well-chronicled Venetian ritual
but its origin is twofold. The birth of the ritual is tied to the exploits of
Doge Pietro Orseolo II, who, on Ascension Day in the year 1000, set
sail from the Lido to battle pirate bands who were terrorising Venetian

trade along the Dalmatian coast. He fought successfully against the pirates and every year thereafter on Ascension Day (the Thursday 40 days after Easter), he decreed that the Doge should return to the Lido port to bless the benevolent waters and pray that they remain calm and quiet for another year. Nearly two centuries later, the ritual became nuptial in nature.

In 1177, Venice played host to rivals Pope Alexander III and Holy Roman Emperor Frederick I. At the conclusion of the treaty that reconciled both sides, Pope Alexander presented Doge Sebastian Ziani with a blessed ring as a symbol of the republic's future supremacy over the sea. This was the first of many rings that the Doge gave to the sea in marriage.

A ceremony of a state leader espousing the sea may sound a bit hackneyed today but it was serious business in the Middle Ages as the merchants of Venice depended on the sea's dowry of trade goods and imports. The ritual was carried out every year with all the pageantry befitting a royal wedding. On Ascension Day, the *Bucintoro* was taken from its slip in the Arsenale to the Molo in front of the Doge's Palace on St. Mark's Square. There, the Doge and the members of the Grand Council, along with any visiting ambassadors or foreign dignitaries, boarded the vessel and set out for the Lido port amid a flotilla of smaller ornate vessels and gondolas carrying military commanders, clergy, nobles, wealthy merchants and anyone else deemed important enough to attend a state wedding. Musicians followed the procession in a series of vessels. Diarist John Evelyn chronicled one such wedding procession in 1645, as quoted in Martin Garrett's *Venice: A Cultural Comparison*:

"[the Doge in his robes of state and the gowned Senators] embarked in their own gloriously painted, carved and gilded Bucintoro, environed and followed by innumerable galleys, gondolas, and boats filled with spectators, some dressed in masquerade; trumpets, music and cannons, filling the whole air with din."

Upon reaching the Lido port, the *Bucintoro* oarsmen, all 168 of them, turned the ship around so that the poop deck faced the open sea. Amid the gathering of watercraft both large and small, the church patriarch of the city pronounced a blessing upon the sea and all who sailed her. The Doge then stepped forward, held the wedding ring out and pronounced, "We marry you, oh sea, in token of our true and perpetual dominion." After that, he threw the ring into the sea amid wild cheering and the firing of guns from the city's defences. The entire procession then returned to the Church of San Nicolo del Lido for a solemn Mass.

The Quest for the Ring

With a tradition that lasted over 600 years, you might think there a sizeable collection of rings at the bottom of the port, but this is not so. Shortly after the ring was cast into the sea, hordes of Venetians would strip off their clothes and dive into the sea in search of the ring. The lucky citizen who found it could keep it and lived rent- and tax-free for one year.

To look at the small, carved model of the *Bucintoro* today, you realise it must have been quite a sight fully outfitted in its day. The final *Bucintoro*, the one depicted in the model, was nearly 45 metres (150 feet) long and 7.6 metres (25 feet) high in the water. It seated 90 on its upper deck and effectively hid 14 dozen oarsmen on a deck below. It was splendidly furnished with every luxury of the day including exotic fabrics from the Middle East and Asia and a gaudy

A side view of the Bucintoro.

display of gilded figures near the prow. As Goethe described, it would have been wrong to call the craft "overladen with ornaments" as "the whole ship is one single ornament."

Seaworthy?

The Adriatic never had any say in the matter of whether or not the Doge was worthy of the sea but one thing is for sure—his ship certainly was not. The *Bucintoro*, for all its decoration, was barely seaworthy. So unstable was the flat-bottomed craft that it could only be used when the waters were calm. One visiting dignitary noted that, without discretion, the marriage of the Doge and the sea might one day be consummated.

The *Bucintoro*, like most things Venetian, came to a sad end. After the fall of the republic to Napoleon in 1797, the ship was looted of its ornaments and gilt. It was converted into a gunboat and finally a prison barge before being scrapped in 1824.

A Lesser Production Today

The Ascension Day tradition (now renamed the Feast of La Sensa) continues to this day, albeit in a more modest form. On Ascension Day, the mayor of Venice, civic, religious and military dignitaries and many others in period costume leave St. Mark's Square in rowed boats for the Lido port, where the mayor casts a ring into the sea.

The Museo Storico Navale houses fascinating exhibits, models and artefacts relating to Venice's long maritime tradition.

Colleoni's Will

Equestrian statue of Bartolomeo Colleoni,
Campo dei Santi Giovanni e Paolo

*A famous and wealthy military commander leaves
his entire estate to the city of Venice, but with an
interesting catch.*

By the end of the 1400s, Venice was an economic powerhouse with an expanding empire. Whenever such assets exist, a means of protecting those interests are sure to follow. Venice was no exception to this rule and, by the 15th century, it had conquered large tracts of northern Italy and most of the eastern Mediterranean. Venice used its own sons to staff the battalions and to sail the galleys for these campaigns whenever possible. However, when commanders ran short, the city reached for the purse and hired professionals. Such professional men of arms, often called *condottieri*, were widely available in medieval Italy. But they did not come cheap. A fact that became clear to Venice as conducting such expansions had left the treasury nearly depleted until a noted condottiere offered a unique solution.

Bartolomeo Colleoni was a military man of the first order who was sought out and employed by the leaders of Naples, Rome and Milan before he accepted a position as general of the Venetian land armies in 1455. A post that he kept for the rest of his life. He was an expert in cavalry movements and a pioneer in the tactics of artillery. He was also quite adept at finance and was able to amass a sizeable fortune while turning down very lucrative offers from France and Rome to defect from Venetian service. When Colleoni died of old age, yet another testament to his skill in the field, in 1475, he left his entire fortune to the city of Venice. It came just in time.

By 1475, Venice was nearly bankrupt from fighting the Turks. The Venetian fleet was badly depleted and with no funds to pay the shipbuilders of the Arsenale, the outlook was bleak. Unpaid seamen held demonstrations in front of the Doge's Palace, demanding back pay. Colleoni's death was sad news to Venice but word of his will filled the republic's leaders with hope. The condottiere bequeathed his entire estate, some 700,000 ducats, to the city of Venice on one condition—they erect an equestrian statue of him in front of St. Mark's. The dilemma was obvious. The city desperately needed the money but to erect a statue in St. Mark's Square was impossible. Not even the saint himself had a statue in the square. After much deliberation, the Senate came up with a novel solution. By parsing the words of his will, they decided to focus on the letter of his request, if not his intent, and decreed that the statue should be erected in front of St. Mark's School in the nearby Campo dei Santi Giovanni e Paolo. It was an interpreted solution to be sure but the Senate deemed the terms of the will to be satisfied. Colleoni's money was deposited into the treasury and an artist was commissioned to begin work on the statue. The Senate chose Andrea Verrocchio of Florence, a sculptor second only to Donatello in his day.

A Master's Master

Verrocchio was the most well-rounded artist of his day, sculpting in stone and wood, casting everything from gold jewellery to bronze cannons and painting for many commissioners. Verrocchio's Florentine workshop was renowned for mastery and innovation and drew many talented apprentices. One of them was a 15-year-old Leonardo da Vinci.

Verrocchio travelled to Venice and set up a workshop where he began the model for the horse. However, the Senate changed its mind about the commission and restricted Verrocchio to only completing the horse; the sculpting of the figure of Colleoni would go to a Venetian artist. When Verrocchio heard news of this, he flew into a rage and broke off the head and forelegs of the model horse, then left Venice for Florence. When the leaders of the Senate received word of Verrocchio's destruction, they dispatched a letter after him advising him not to return to Venice or they would cut off his head. Unfazed, Verrocchio sent a

Colleoni is best remembered for Verrocchio's bronze equestrian statue that stands in the Campo dei Santi Giovanni e Paolo.

reply stating that he would take care not to return to Venice for once the Senate leaders decreed that a man's head should be cut off, they had no way to replace it and they certainly could not replace a head like his. He, however, could replace a horse's head and with one that was even more beautiful than the original.

The Senate was quite taken with Verrocchio's response and rescinded the death sentence, doubled his fee and gave him control over the entire project. Verrocchio returned to Venice to complete the work but died just before it was cast.

Uniform Praise

Verrocchio's statue is arguably one of the greatest equestrian sculptures in the world. Noted Venetian architectural scholar John Ruskin said of it in his treatise *The Stones of Venice*: "I do not believe that there is a more glorious work of sculpture existing in the world." English novelist Henry James described the statue in *The Aspern Papers* thus, "and looking up at the small square-jawed face of Bartolomeo Colleoni, the terrible condottiere who sits so sturdily astride his huge bronze horse, on the high pedestal on which Venetian gratitude maintains him. The statue is incomparable, the finest of all mounted figures…"

INSIDER'S TIPS

Church of Santi Giovanni e Paolo This large brick church, along with the Frari and St. Mark's, is one of the principal churches in the city. More than the other two churches, this church is a warehouse for the doges of Venice as 25 of them have tombs of various sizes inside the church's cavernous interior. Bellini and Veronese also have works within. Euro 3. Open 7.30am–12.30pm, 3.30pm–7.30pm Monday to Saturday, 3pm–6pm Sunday. Campo dei Santi Giovanni e Paolo.

Monument to Colleoni The mounted cavalier dominates the campo from his high vantage. Campo dei Santi Giovanni e Paolo.

Scuola of San Giorgio delgi Schiavoni This out-of-the-way and fairly modest building houses some true treasures of Venice in a collection of nine paintings by Carpaccio. If you liked the Carpaccios in the Gallerie dell'Accademia, take in these as well. Euro 3. Open 9.30am–12.30pm, 3.30pm–6.30pm Tuesday to Saturday, 9.30am–12.30pm Sunday (April to October); 10am–12.30pm, 3pm–6pm Tuesday to Saturday, 10am–noon Sunday (November to March). Closed Monday. Calle dei Furlani.

Museo Storico Navale (Naval History Museum) Venice has a very rich naval history, which is beautifully recorded in this interesting museum. Of interest are the *Bucintoro* model in Room 16 and the amazing seashell collection (called the Swedish Collection) on the top floor. Euro 1.55. Open 8.45am–1.30pm Monday to Friday, 8.45am–1pm Saturday. Closed Sunday. Campo San Biagio.

Torri dell'Arsenale (Arsenale Gates) These gates are a wonderful example of Renaissance fortifications in Venice. Campo Arsenale.

Church of Santa Maria della Visitazione (La Pietà) This is the church where Vivaldi taught and where he composed some of his greatest works including *The Four Seasons*. There are also some impressive works by Tiepolo inside. Free. Open daily 10am–noon, 1pm–6pm. Riva degli Schiavoni.

Church of Santa Maria Formosa This church, situated in one of Venice's most picturesque squares, has a couple of nice Vivarini paintings and a Palma the Younger. Euro 2.50 or Chorus Pass. Open 10am–5pm Monday to Saturday, 1pm–5pm Sunday. Campo Santa Maria Formosa.

Church of San Zaccaria This parish church hosts a lovely Bellini and a Tintoretto in the Cappella. The crypt (a rarity in waterlogged Venice) houses the tombs of eight doges. Free (Euro 1 to enter the Cappella and the crypt). Open 10am–noon, 4pm–6pm Monday to Saturday, 4pm–6pm Sunday. Campo Zaccaria.

Liassidi Palace Situated in the old Liassidi Palace, this four-star gem delivers like a five-star. This is what palace living in old Venice must have really been like. The Liassidi is truly decadent. Doubles between Euro 130–520. Suites between Euro 180–1200. 3405 Ponte dei Greci. Tel: 041 5205658. Website: www. www.liassidipalacehotel.com

Hotel Paganelli This three-star hotel right on the Riva is an affordable alternative to the more expensive Danieli and Gabrieli hotels. The interior decor looks like a hip throwback to the 1960s but the staff is nice and the price is right. Doubles between Euro 120–240. Riva degli Schiavoni. Tel: 041 5224324. Website: www.hotelpaganelli.com

La Residenza This is a very nice two-star hotel situated inside an old palazzo on a picturesque campo. All rooms have a bath and air conditioning. Singles between Euro 50–100. Doubles between Euro 80–160. 3608 Campo Bandiera e Moro. Tel: 041 5285315. Website: www.venicelaresidenza.com

Hotel Al Piave This family-oriented three-star hotel is located halfway between the Campo Santa Maria Formosa (one of Venice's most beautiful squares) and the Campo San Zaccaria. Doubles with bath between Euro 100–185 and multi-room family suites between Euro 200–265. English-language babysitting available. Ruga Giuffa. Tel: 041 5285174. Website: www.hotelalpiave.com

Locanda Giovanni e Paolo A great little three-star hotel with big charm next to the Church of Santi Giovanni e Paolo. Singles with bathroom between Euro 50–110. Doubles with bathroom between Euro 80–180. Barbaria delle Tole. Tel: 041 5222767. Website: www.locandassgiovannipaolo.it

Trattoria Al Scalinetto This little *trattoria* offers great traditional Venetian fare at a fair price. Dishes between Euro 8–15. Get there by 7.30pm or call ahead to make sure you get in. South of Campo Bandiera e Moro. Tel: 041 5200776.

Corte Sconta This is one of the better restaurants in this area so a reservation is recommended as it is nearly always full. Dishes between Euro 10–15. Calle del Pestrin. Tel: 041 5227024.

Birreria alla Strega This welcoming place is one of the few to serve a truly refreshing combination for travellers— hot pizza and cold beer. Cheap and informal. Corte della Terraza.

Rosa Salva This is the best *gelateria* (ice-cream shop) in Venice with all the *gelato* made in-house. It is also a fantastic *pasticceria* (pastry shop/café). A pastry shop has been in this location on the campo for over 250 years now and it's easy to see why. Campo dei Santi Giovanni e Paolo. Tel: 041 5227949.

Giovanna Zanella Giovanna runs a custom shoe and purse shop in her small studio. She makes all of her unique designs right in the shop. Good-quality and innovative designs. Wear what no one else is wearing this year. Calle Carnimati (near Campo S. Lio). Tel: 041 5235500.

Flavia Do Carnival right by renting a period costume from Flavia. She also allows you try on costumes and take photos for a small fee. Campo S. Lio. Tel: 041 5287429. Website: www.veniceatelier.com

Venetian Navigator A small internet point between San Marco and the Rialto. Calle Cassellaria. Tel: 041 2771056. Website: www. venetiannavigator.com

Internet Corner Apparently the only internet café in northern Castello. (Well, the only one I could find.) Open 10am–10pm. Closed Sunday. Calle Barbaria delle Tole.

Short Walk

Starting Point—Church of Santi Giovanni e Paolo. This is one of the largest churches in Venice and is home to the tombs of 25 doges. Take time to look at Colleoni's statue in the campo before moving on. Walk along Salizz. SS. Giovanni e Paolo and turn right into Calle d. Ospedale. Cross the two canals and veer right onto Calle Lunga Santa Maria Formosa. This will lead you into the Campo Santa Maria Formosa, which is surrounded by a number of beautiful palaces. Linger here a while as this is a true treasure and not mentioned in many guidebooks. Take Ruga Giuffa south out of the campo and follow it as it turns into C. Corte Rotta. Turn right into the narrow Campo San Provolo, which will lead into the larger Campo San Zaccaria with its church. The church has a crypt (an interesting touch in Venice) containing the tombs of eight doges. From this campo, exit south to the Riva delgi Schiavoni, Venice's premier waterfront promenade. Follow this east (away from San Marco) until you cross the Rio dell'Arsenale into the Campo San Biagio. This is where you will find the Museo Storico Navale (not to be missed). The unique entrance to the Arsenale is just up from the campo.

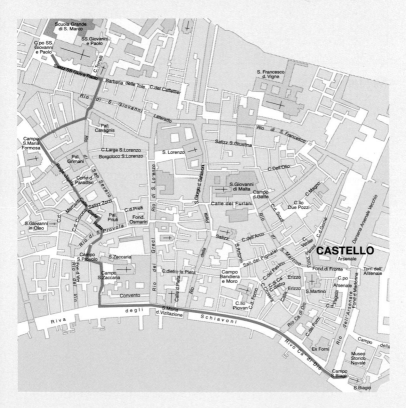

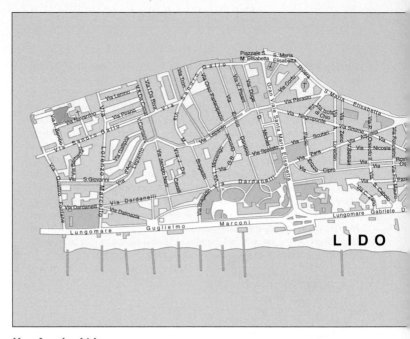

Key for the Lido

1. Church of San Nicolo
2. Porto di Lido

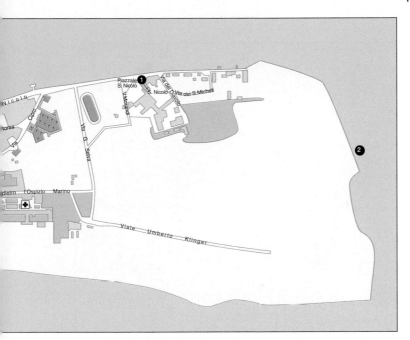

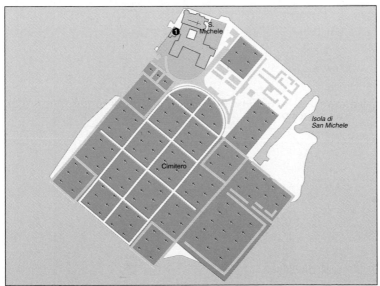

Key for the Island of San Michele
1. Cemetery

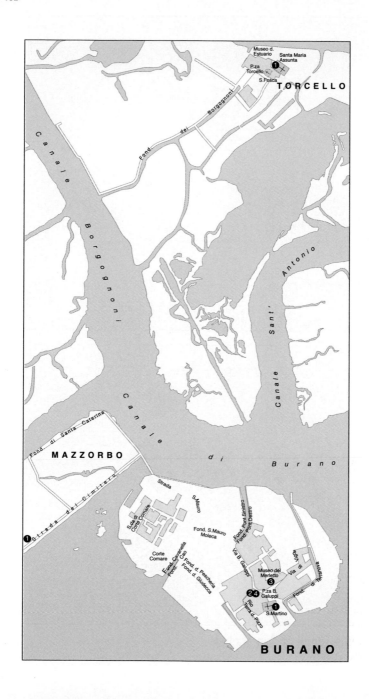

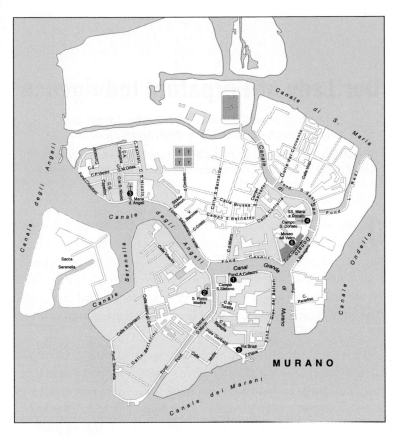

Key for Murano
1. Busa alla Torre
2. Church of San Pietro Martire
3. Church of Santa Maria degli Angeli
4. Church of Santi Maria e Donato
5. Locanda Al Soffiador
6. Museo del Vetro (Glass Museum)

Key for Burano
1. Church of San Martino
2. Hotel Raspo de Ua
3. Museo del Merletto
   (Lace Museum)
4. Trattoria Raspo de Ua

Key for Mazzorbo
1. Church of Santa Caterina del Mazzorbo

Key for Torcello
1. Cathedral of Santa Maria Assunta

Our Lady of Perpetual Indulgence

Church of Santa Caterina del Mazzorbo, Mazzorbo,
and Church of Santa Maria degli Angeli, Murano

*The convents and nunneries of a city are supposed to be places of piety
and chastity but it was not always the case in Renaissance Venice.*

During the Renaissance in Venice, women generally had three destinies available to them: become a wife, become a nun or become a whore. Any woman not married or in a convent was considered by society to be in peril of defaulting to the third destiny. Women of the time needed the protection of the husband or the convent lest they fall prey to the same fate as a prostitute. However, history records many cases in which the convent did not provide any protection.

Venetian history is coloured with many examples of sexual misconduct, excessive sexual licence (compared to other cities in Italy) and sexual conquest but you would think the convents and nunneries of the city immune to such baseness. But even in these holy corners of Venice—"the sea-Sodom", as Lord Byron called it— history provides some examples of debauchery, including the priest and convent master Giovanni Leon who was executed on the Molo, the small dock in front of the Doge's Palace, in 1561 for extorting sexual favours from the nuns of Le Convertite (now converted to a prison for women) and the nuns of San Zaccaria convent (now only the church remains) who cut a hole in the wall of the convent to allow their lovers access. Other such examples exist but many of the convents mentioned in the Venetian state archives have long since closed and their buildings torn down or converted to other uses. Others are mentioned only in anonymity. However, there are two convents that were mentioned specifically, both of which still exist today (although the convents themselves have been closed), hidden away as it were in the outer islands of the lagoon north of Venice.

The unassuming and quaint Church of Santa Caterina del Mazzorbo belies its colourful past.

Santa Caterina del Mazzorbo rests on the remote island of Mazzorbo. Reached either by boat or via the wooden footbridge from the lace island of Burano, Mazzorbo was once a thriving port. It would have continued to thrive had Venice not grown into the giant it was. Of the many homes, shops and estates on the island, only a few survive. Another survivor is the church and nearby cloister of Santa Caterina del Mazzorbo. Built in 1263, it is one of the oldest standing buildings in the lagoon. Its interesting wooden 'boat keel' roof is typical of medieval Venetian church construction. The cloister closed in the 1800s but it once was the talk of Venice when, in 1613, a group of young noblemen were denounced for their nocturnal visits to Santa Caterina del Mazzorbo. The denunciation stated: "They go into the parlour next to the church, and to the doors of the convent, where they remain for a long time exchanging dishonest word with the said nuns, as if they were in a public bordello."

The comparison of convents to bordellos was common practice at the time. Mary Laven, a noted author on the subject, describes numerous examples such as the Franciscan priest in 1497 who preached at St. Mark's that "whenever a foreign gentleman comes to this city, they show him the nunneries, scarcely nunneries at all in fact but brothels and public bordellos" and the 16th-century writer who called the city's nuns "public prostitutes" and that the "honest whore-houses", as he called them, should be burned down for the good of the Venetian state.

Casanova Enters the Convent

One Venetian who knew something of bordellos, Casanova, apparently knew something of convents too if we are to believe his autobiography. Casanova was a regular visitor to the Church of Santa Maria degli Angeli on the glass island of Murano, where he went to the adjoining convent to visit his lover Caterina Capretta, who was confined to the cloister, pregnant with his child. Another of the nuns from the convent, no angel herself as she already had one lover, fell in love with Casanova and endeavoured to have him. This nun, known only to us from Casanova's cryptic acronym M.M.,  was able to leave the confines of the convent at night and would meet her famous lover in the garden next to the church for a night of carnal delights.

Men who courted the nuns of Venice became so brazen that the city authorities were forced to act. Interestingly, little legislation had existed at the beginning of the Renaissance against the sexual relations with nuns. After all, this was a crime, a sex crime, against God as nuns were betrothed to Christ as his brides upon their entry into a convent. Further, any man who seduced or raped a nun was quite literally making a cuckold of Christ. Little wonder no such laws existed; the senators and counsellors of the day probably did not dream that Christian men would consider partaking in such an atrocity. It did not take them long to lay down the law.

Predators

Men pursuing and courting nuns became so common during the Renaissance period that a new word was invented to describe such men. They were called *Monachini*, or "the nun chasers".

The first laws provided for lifelong banishment from the city for a man who engaged in sexual congress with a nun, 10 years' banishment for a man who unlawfully visited a convent and six months in jail for any gondolier who ferried such a man to his destination. However, this did little to quell the illicit liaisons between nuns and the laity so stronger legislation was enacted. This time, the punishment was death as decreed by the Council of Ten in 1605:

"And if anyone in the future, whoever he may be, excepting those who are admitted by the laws, is found inside a convent, or is accused of having been inside by day or night, even if he is not convicted of carnal commerce, once he is arrested and the truth has been ascertained, let his head be cut off so that it is separated from the body, and so that death ensues."

With this increased legislation, little more was heard from the convents on such matters; the days of 'perpetual indulgence' were over in Venice.

Saving Venice

Porto di Lido, Lido

Venice is sinking and an ambitious project to hold back the sea may be its only hope.

"Venice, lost and won, her thirteen hundred years of freedom done, sinks like a sea-weed into whence she rose," wrote Lord Byron in Childe Harold's Pilgrimage. *Although Lord Byron's prediction has yet to come true, the future of Venice depends on preventing the Adriatic's waters from carrying away the city.*

Venice is a city under silent siege. The waters of the Adriatic, the very sea that lifted Venice to a world power, are now threatening to undermine and overwhelm it. Sixteen hundred years ago, when the city was founded, the water level was more than 1.5 metres

(5 feet) lower than it is today. And that same water level is predicted to rise an estimated 12 to 91 centimetres (5 to 36 inches) by the end of this century. High tides, or *acqua alte* as the locals call them, have been a part of Venetian life for centuries but the phenomenon of daily flooding in the city is getting dramatically worse. In the early part of the 20th century, St. Mark's Square flooded only six or seven times a year. By 1990, that number had risen to 40 times a year. By 1996, it was 99 times. In 2002, it was 110 times. Venice is sinking and an ambitious project to control the fickle tides of the Adriatic might be its only hope.

The union between Venice and the sea has often been a tumultuous one. Built up over 1000 years from 118 separate small islands in its own protected lagoon, Venice literally sprang up from the sea. In the 5th century, refugees from the surrounding mainland migrated to the islets in the Venetian lagoon in order to escape the plundering wrath of Attila the Hun. The difficult, waterlogged conditions in the lagoon discouraged Attila's pursuit. These refugees, and several other waves over the next 100 years, reclaimed marshland from the brackish waters of the lagoon, shored up softer soils and created permanent foundations for the fledgling city. Some reclamation projects worked; others foundered. Yet in time, the modern city of Venice took shape on the water. Fishing, shipbuilding and seaborne commerce fed the city and eventually enriched it to the ornate jewel it is today. The Adriatic provided both shelter and sustenance for Venice but now the relationship is souring. But what has caused the sea, the life of Venice, to turn on the city?

Building on the Sea

Venice's unique location and land- and seascape mandated a different form of construction from other medieval and Renaissance Italian cities. Foundations in Venice are formed by driving piles made of pine 7 to 8 metres (23 to 26 feet) deep into the mud until they strike the hard clay under the lagoon. More traditional brick foundations are then laid, upon which buildings can be erected. The delicate nature of these pile-based foundations require that Venetian buildings are constructed with lighter materials and are only raised to a modest height.

The acqua alte at the north end of the near closed Adriatic tend to be more pronounced than in other parts of the gulf. This is due in part to a unique combination of geography and meteorology, which is usually manifested during the winter months. During the winter, the area around Venice is often covered with low-pressure weather systems. With such weather systems come tidal surges in the same way that low-pressure hurricanes or cyclones create tidal surges. Compound this low-pressure phenomenon with the fact that high-pressure areas seek to find low-pressure areas via the path of least resistance (in this case the Adriatic) and you have prevailing southeasterly winds, known as siroccos, sweeping up the entire fetch of the gulf towards Venice. When you have both of these phenomena coupled with the daily cycles of the tides, you get acqua alte.

St. Mark's Square, the lowest part of the city, is always the first area affected by an acqua alta. Nearly all of Venice's drains are interconnected and empty into the Grand Canal. So when it rains in Venice, a good portion of the water drains to the lowest part of the city. The bad news is that when the tides rise, water flows back up through the drains and the waters percolate into St. Mark's Square. Most people assume that the water simply rushes into the square over the banks of the Grand Canal. While this can and does happen, during extremely high tides the square will already be flooded via the drains. During unusually high tides (measuring 1 metre (3.28 feet) or more), as much as 70% of the city can be inundated. Fortunately, these dangerous floods are rare and the routine acqua alte are regarded as nothing more than a nuisance during which visitors to St. Mark's Square are forced to walk along narrow raised wooden planks called *passarelle*. These passarelle also extend into the basilica itself, the interior of which floods in concert with the square. For those who wish to venture off the passarelle, many shops around the piazza sell rubber overboots. When exceptionally high tides do occur, a siren is sounded throughout the city, which is exactly what happened on 4 November 1966.

In the early part of November 1966, the normal acqua alta combination of low atmospheric pressure and sirocco winds was

A nonchalant man wades through a flooded St. Mark's Square.

exacerbated by abnormally heavy rainfall. The result was the worst flood in Venice's history in which St. Mark's Square was covered by more than 1.5 metres (5 feet) of water. The high waters caused massive damage throughout the city and burst the city's fuel storage tanks, leaving the city awash in black petroleum. This flood and one almost as bad the next year served as a wake-up call to Italy and to the world that Venice was in trouble. Aid began to pour into the city from other European countries and UNESCO began to aid in Venetian repairs and restoration. But these were only stopgap measures against the ever-worsening threat from the sea.

Since the late 1960s, research has been done to determine how best to control the tides of the Adriatic within the lagoon. The most widely accepted way of protecting the city was with a tidal barrier that could be engaged only when the waters were at their highest. Such a system would protect the city when in danger but would allow for a normal tidal cycle within the lagoon to ensure the waterway's natural ecosystem would be protected. In the mid-1980s, after much modelling and simulation, a prototype was towed into place at the Porto di Lido at the north end of Lido island. The project, nicknamed MOSES for the larger name Modulo Sperimentale Elettromecanico and likened to the biblical Moses who parted and held back the Red Sea, would consist of 79 interlocking steel flaps that would lie flat on the sea floor at the three openings to the lagoon and which could be raised by inflating them with air to create a barrier against an acqua alta.

The project has its proponents and opponents in a typically Italian chorus of political discord and the on again-off again project has been scuttled and resurrected numerous times. Finally, in May 2003, Italian President Silvio Berlusconi officially launched the MOSES project, which is expected to be completed in 2011 at a cost of Euro 6 billion. Yet the question persists: Will the gates protect the city from the sea? Only time will tell.

Many Ideas

There has been no shortage of ideas about how to save sinking Venice. These have ranged from the selected MOSES floodgates project to ideas such as creating artificial breakwaters or pumping 180 million cubic metres (6,357 million cubic feet) of water back into an underground aquifer to combat the effects of years of subsidence.

The Island of Glass

Museo del Vetro (Glass Museum), Murano

Glass is so common today that we scarcely give it a second thought. Yet there was a time when the manufacture of this once-rare material was a closely guarded state secret.

As an economic and trading giant of its day, Venice traded in goods from northern Europe to the far reaches of Asia. Consisting of shrewd businessmen, Venice knew precisely which products to trade in and which ones to manufacture. For instance, Venetians only traded in Asian silks and Persian carpets, knowing full well that they could never compete in the manufacture of such products. Yet the city was quick to see a lucrative opportunity when it came to the rare and esoteric art of medieval glass crafting. Furthermore, it knew exactly how to control its monopoly.

At the Museo del Vetro, or Glass Museum, on the island of Murano, you can explore the history of glass and glassmaking in the area of Venice. According to several of its exhibits, glass in the area dates back to Roman times. However, the first evidence of glassmaking in the city dates to a document written at the end of the first millennium in which a Benedictine monk describes making glass bottles for use in the home. The nascent glass industry in the lagoon got a much-needed boost when Venice pushed its exclusive trade routes into Egypt, Syria and other Islamic ports in the Eastern Mediterranean, all of which had long traditions of glass blowing. This knowledge was brought back to Venice, where the glassworkers quickly formed a trade guild in which they committed to conserving their knowledge.

The scattered glass furnaces of Venice increased in number as the industry grew. Yet as Venice was at that time a city constructed almost entirely of wood and its citizens lived in constant fear of fire, the entire glass industry was moved to the nearby island of Murano in 1291. It was not the first time that a 'dangerous' industry or facility had been isolated in the lagoon. The initial metal foundries located where the Jewish Ghetto is today were moved to the safety of the Arsenale in the 1100s and hospitals treating contagious diseases were moved to the islands of Lazzaretto Vecchio and Lazzaretto Nuovo following the first plague outbreak in 1348. The change to the sleepy island of Murano was profound as it became home to several hundred furnaces and quickly developed into what was to be the glass capital of Europe for nearly five centuries.

Poison-Proof Glassware?

Murano crystal glassware gained such a reputation for being so finely made that it was believed that any trace of poison introduced to a liquid contained therein would cause the glass to shatter. Whether true or not, it was marketing genius as paranoid nobles throughout Europe demanded the protection of Murano glass.

The Murano craftsmen perfected all types of glass crafting such as crystal, mirrors, lenses for spectacles, beads, artworks and faux glass gemstones (the making of the latter became outlawed as the imitations appeared so authentic that even professionals of the day were fooled). There is even a record of an entire set of glass furniture being made. The skill of the Murano glassworkers became the stuff of legend throughout Europe as detailed by an English doctor who chronicled a visit to a Murano furnace in 1781:

"I saw a very fine plate [of glass], for a mirror...Instead of being cast, as in France and England, the Murano mirrors are all blown in the same manner of bottles. It is astonishing to see with what dexterity the workman wields a long hollow cylinder of melted glass, at the end of an iron tube, which, when he has extended as much as possible, by blowing, and every other means his art suggests, he slits with a sharp instrument, removing the two extremities from each other, and folding

A simple yet elegant piece of Murano glassware.

back the sides: the cylinder now appears as a large sheet of glass, which being once more introduced into the furnace, is brought out a clear, finished plate."

The glass workers of Murano quickly became the island's leading citizens and enjoyed many privileges. The Venetian government afforded them these privileges in the attempt to keep the invaluable glassmakers in Venice, thus keeping their knowledge confined to the lagoon. Glassworkers were allowed to carry swords in the city and the daughters of glassmakers were allowed to marry into the noble families of Venice. This had long-lasting consequences as it meant that the children of the union would be noble as well, a thing unheard of in the rest of Venetian society. There is even substantial evidence that these workers enjoyed widespread immunity from criminal persecution, which seems substantiated by Casanova, who chronicled being stranded on a dock in Murano at night with a heavy purse:

"I had reason to fear the robbers of Murano, very dangerous and determined cutthroats who enjoy and abuse a number of privileges which the policy of the government grants them in return for the work they do in the glass factories with which the island abounds; to keep them from emigrating the government grants all of them Venetian citizenship."

These liberties proved enough of an enticement for most of the craftsmen to stay. For those who dared to stray from the city of St. Mark, a slate of dire consequences awaited. First, any émigré was branded a traitor and arrested and his home and possessions confiscated by the

A dying trade—modern-day glassmakers on the island of Murano.

state. Others had their hands cut off while those who did manage to escape to other regions were routinely hunted down by assassins. In this manner of afforded liberty and stern reprisals, Venice was able to control the glass trade as a virtual monopoly well into the 17th century.

An Industry in Trouble

Today's Murano glassworks may be a dying breed as many are facing financial hard times in the face of cheaper foreign competition. One local outlet even markets foreign manufactured goods made to look like authentic Murano glass! To make matters worse, few Venetian boys want to undergo the long and difficult apprenticeship required to become a master glass blower in an industry with such an uncertain future. Traditional Murano is not faring well in the global economy as hardly any of the remaining furnaces on the island are locally or even Italian owned.

INSIDER'S TIPS

Cemetery Island of San Michele Normally a cemetery would not be included in a city guidebook, but this is Venice. Stop off here on your way to Murano. Free. Open 7.30am–6pm April to September; 7.30am–4pm October to March. Island of San Michele.

Church of San Pietro Martire Just off Murano's Grand Canal, this church is worth a visit if you are on the island. It contains works by Bellini and Veronese. Free. Open daily 9am–noon, 3pm–6pm. Fondamenta da Mula (Murano).

Church of Santi Maria e Donato This ancient church on Murano dates back to the 7th century. The mosaics, for which the church is famous, date back to when the church was reconstructed in the 12th century. Of interest are the four large rib bones hanging behind the altar, they are the supposed remnants of a dragon slain by St. Donato. Free. Open 9am–noon, 3.30pm–7pm Monday to Saturday, 3.30pm–7pm Sunday. Campo San Donato (Murano).

Santa Maria degli Angeli This church is located on Murano. Open only for Mass. Fondamenta Sebastiano Venier (Murano).

Museo del Vetro (Glass Museum) Located on Murano, this interesting little museum explores the history of glass in the lagoon from the time of the Romans to the 18th century. Euro 4, reduced to Euro 2.50 with VENICECard. Open 10am–4pm (November to March); 10am–5pm (April to October). Ticket office closes one hour before closing. Closed Wednesday. Fondamenta Giustinian 8 (Murano). Tel: 041 739586. Website: www.museiciviciveneziani.it/main.asp?lin=EN

Church of San Martino The only church on the island of Burano, San Martino is distinctly local with its leaning tower. There is a lovely Tiepolo painting inside. Free. Open daily 8am–noon, 3pm–7pm. Piazza Galuppi (Burano).

Museo del Merletto (Lace Museum) This museum follows the history of the island's relationship with the manufacture of lace. Check out this museum before you go shopping on the island so that you can distinguish foreign (mass-produced) lace from the local genuine article. Euro 4, reduced to Euro 2.50 with VENICECard. Open 10am–4pm (November to March); 10am–5pm (April to October). Ticket office closes one hour before closing. Closed Tuesday. Piazza Galuppi (Burano). Tel: 041 730034. Website: www.museicivicivenezian. it/main.asp?lin=EN

Church of Santa Caterina del Mazzorbo Free. Open 9am–noon Friday to Sunday. Mazzorbo.

Cathedral of Santa Maria Assunta This is the oldest standing building in the Venetian lagoon, dating back to 639. It is renowned for its Byzantine mosaics. Euro 3. Open daily 10.30am–6pm. Torcello.

Church of San Nicolo This church was built to house the mortal remains of St. Nicholas, which were reportedly stolen from the port of Bari by Venetians. Free. Open daily 8am–noon, 3pm–7pm. Riviera San Nicolo (Lido).

Locanda Al Soffiador Located just behind Murano's lighthouse, this is a great little B&B-style hotel. Doubles with bath from Euro 60. 11 Viale Bressaggio (Murano). Website: http://alsoffiador.hotel-venezia.net

Hotel Raspo de Ua This small seven-room hotel is the only option on Burano. Singles without bath from Euro 40. Doubles with bath from Euro 75. 560 Via Galuppi (Burano). Tel: 041 730095.

Busa alla Torre A great Murano fresh seafood restaurant. Campo San Stefano (Murano). Tel: 041 739662.

Trattoria Raspo de Ua This *trattoria*, associated with Hotel Raspo de Ua, consistently gets good reviews. 560 Via Galuppi (Burano). Tel: 041 730095.

Short Walk

This is not so much a walk as it is a series of short walks broken up by boat rides to reach the islands. **Starting Point**—Fondamenta Nuove in Cannaregio. Catch either Vaporetto 41 or 42 to the peaceful cemetery island of San Michele. Isolated behind high brick walls and cypress trees, you can find the final resting places of such greats as Ezra Pound and Igor Stravinsky. Once you have finished here, catch the northbound 41 or 42 to Murano.

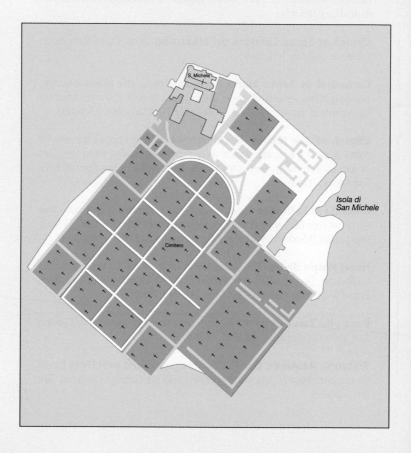

Get off the Vaporetto at the stop for Colonna and walk along the Fondamenta dei Vetrai with its many glass furnaces until you reach Murano's Grand Canal. Cross the bridge (Ponte Vivarini) over to the Fondamenta Cavour and follow it until you reach the Museo del Vetro (Glass Museum). Retrace your steps back to the Fondamenta dei Vetrai. Cross the bridge and turn left onto the Fondamenta D. Manin. Walk along this street until you come to the Viale Galibaldi. Turn left onto this street and follow it until you reach the Faro Vaporetto stop. Continue on to Burano via Vaporetto 12 or the LN Vaporetto.

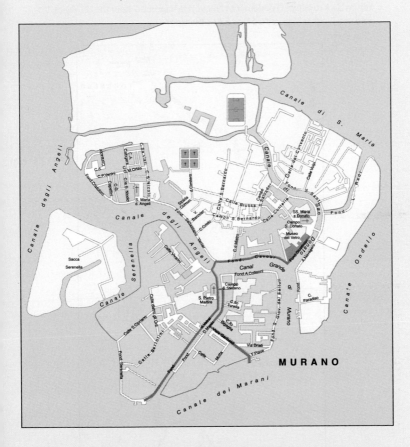

Alight at the stop for Burano and walk towards the Fondamenta S. Mauro, which will turn into Via B. Galuppi, with its many lace shops. This street eventually turns into Piazza B. Galuppi, which contains the island's lace museum (Museo del Merletto). Retrace your steps back to the Burano Vaporetto stop, where you can catch a shuttle boat to the nearby and secluded island of Torcello, with its aged Church of Santa Maria Assunta. Alternatively, from the Burano stop, you can easily walk over to the quiet fishing village of Mazzorbo and visit its church, Santa Caterina, which can be found along the Strada del Cimitero. From Burano, return back to Venice (Fondamenta Nuove) via Vaporetto 12 or the LN Vaporetto and catch either Vaporetto 51 or 52 to the Lido.

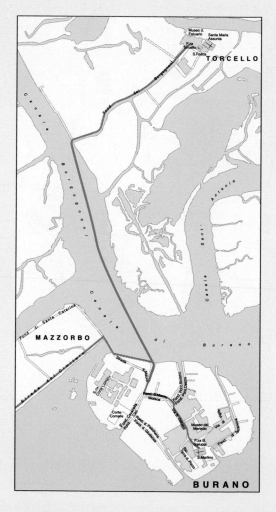

Get off at the stop for S. Maria Elisabetta. One word of warning about walking around on the Lido—cars. Yes, that's right, there are cars on the Lido and many a tourist has been clipped by a motorist after getting used to walking around in the vehicle-less environment of Venice. There are really only three interesting places on the Lido. First, San Nicolo, the church dedicated to St. Nicholas (yes, the Santa Claus St. Nick). It is one of the oldest in the lagoon and is less than 1 mile along the Riviera San Nicolo from the Vaporetto stop. Next, the Jewish cemeteries on Via Cipro are halfway between San Nicolo and the Vaporetto stop. Finally, the only other place worth visiting on the Lido is the beach. (Yes, the beach. Remember that Venice is in a lagoon, the outer bank of the Lido faces the Adriatic Sea.) It is accessible via the Gran Viale Santa Maria Elisabetta.

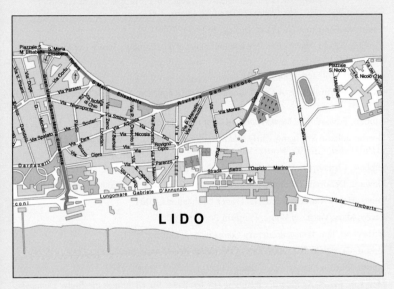

Bibliography

English Sources

Byron, Lord George Gordon. *Childe Harold's Pilgrimage*. Kessinger Publishing, 2004.

Calimani, Riccardo. *The Ghetto of Venice*. M. Evans, 1987.

Casanova, Giacomo. *History of My Life*. Putnam, 1959.

Cipriani, Arrigo. *Harry's Bar: The Life and Times of the Legendary Venice Landmark*. Arcade Publishing, 1996.

Dante. *Inferno*. Signet Book, 2001.

Garrett, Martin. *Venice: A Cultural and Literary Companion*. Interlink Publishing Group, 2001.

Gibbon, Edward. *The Memoirs of the Life of Edward Gibbon*. Methuen, 1900.

Goethe, Johann Wolfgang. *Early and Miscellaneous Letters of J.W. Goethe Including Letters to His Mother*. Camden House, 1884.

Hibbert, Christopher. *Venice: The Biography of a City*. W.W. Norton, 1989.

Howard, Deborah. *The Architectural History of Venice*. Yale University Press, 2002.

James, Henry. *The Aspern Papers*. Dover Publications, 2001.

Laven, Mary. *Virgins of Venice*. Penguin Books, 2003.

Littlewood, Ian. *Venice: A Literary Companion*. J. Murray, 1991.

Mason, Georgina. *The Courtesans of the Italian Renaissance*. St. Martin's Press, 1976.

Moore, John. *A View of Society and Manners of Italy*. J. Smith, 1803.

Moryson, Fynes. *An Itinerary Including His Ten Yeeres Travell through the Twelve Dominions of Germany, Bohmerland, Sweitzerland, Netherland, Denmarke, Poland, Italy, Turky, France, England, Scotland and Ireland*. MacMillan, 1907.

Norwich, John Julius. *Paradise of Cities: Venice in the 19th Century*. Doubleday, 2003.

Norwich, John Julius. *A History of Venice*. Knopf, 1982.

Perocco, Guido. *The Horses of San Marco*. Olivetti, 1979.

Petrarch, Francesco. *Selections from the Canzoniere and Other Works*. Oxford University Press, 1999.

Pullan, Brian. *The Jews of Europe and the Inquisition of Venice: 1550–1670*. Barnes & Noble Imports, 1983.

Rosenthal, Margaret F. *The Honest Courtesan*. University of Chicago Press, 1993.

Royal Academy of Arts. *Living Bridges: The Inhabited Bridge, Past, Present and Future*. Prestel, 1997.

Ruskin, John. *The Stones of Venice*. Da Capo Press, 2003.

Sitwell, Osbert. *Winters of Content: And Other Discursions on Mediterranean Art and Travel*. Greenwood Press, 1978.

Twain, Mark. *The Innocents Abroad*. Dover Publications, 2003.

Vasari, Giorgio. *The Lives of the Artists*. Penguin, 1987.

Walker, Frank. *The Man Verdi*. University of Chicago Press, 1982.

Wills, Garry. *Venice Lion City: The Religion of Empire*. Washington Square Press, 2002.

Italian Sources

Favretti, Elvira. *Rime e Lettere di Veronica Franco*. Giornale Storico di Letteratura Italiana 1986.

Tassini, Giuseppe. *Curiosita Veneziane*. Press Venice, 1990.

About the Author

 D. Eric Maikranz began his writing career with the *Denver Post* and later moved to Italy as a correspondent for UPI. Once there, he fell in love with Italy. His passion and interest for the beautiful cities of Italy flourished and he later accepted a position as an English-language tour guide. Maikranz's short fiction has won awards in the United States and his next novel is due to be published in 2005. He splits his time between the United States and Italy.

Index